The Anger Management Workbook for Women

The Problem with Being an Angry Woman and How to Fix it -
Includes 19 Practical Strategies to Master Your Emotions

Victoria Tyler

Table of Contents

Introduction

W hen males grow enraged, no one notices, but when a woman's temper flares, it becomes front-page news. Women's violence is on the increase, with more women being charged for domestic abuse than ever before. So, why have women become enraged? It may simply be because today's females are subjected to growing levels of pressure and responsibilities. Holding your feelings in can, however, lead to your anger building up and exploding at inopportune times. Do you often feel a rage of anger and aggressiveness that takes over everything you are doing? Do you catch yourself losing your temper for every little thing because you do not know how to handle this feeling? Do you resort to physical abuse when this happens? Or perhaps choose to isolate yourself or lock yourself in a room for a while until this feeling passes and you are ready to face people again? Does this happen more times than you can count? Has this, at any point in your life, caused you to lose someone you love or lose an opportunity you wanted badly? Do you often tell yourself you will change but do not know where to begin? From journaling to permanent life changes, this book has all the information you need to start taking control of this dangerous emotion. This book will guide you through the tiny adjustments you must make RIGHT NOW. From different CBT (cognitive behavioral therapy) to breathing techniques, this book has everything you need to know about anger often experienced by women. If you are wondering how anger is different in women and in men, this book covers that too.

When someone opposes what you believe to be correct, anger is a normal feeling. Anger affects people of all ages and cultures, but how you respond to it differs dramatically from one person to the next. When anger becomes a problem, you may find yourself suppressing unpleasant thoughts, venting your frustrations on others, and, in some situations, behaving irresponsibly or doing something you regret later. Setting limits in relationships may be difficult for women, which can contribute to aggressive reactions. This is when you'll need tactics for expressing your rage appropriately because anger is not an emotion to be ignored. This workbook is designed for women who want to feel more in control of their anger and communicate it in a healthy way. This book is going to allow you to learn about the nature and meaning of anger, as well as practical tactics and recommendations for recognizing triggers, managing your reactions, and improving your communication and emotional well-being. You are going to gain this much-awaited emotional control through practical and easy tips, worksheets, and principles you can integrate into your daily life. Failure to regulate your anger may result in a range of issues, including saying things you later regret, shouting at your children, threatening co-workers, sending negligent emails, growing health ailments, and even turning to physical abuse. However, not all cases of aggressiveness are as extreme as this. Alternatively, you may waste time worrying about distressing occurrences, get annoyed in traffic, or venting about work. Learning to manage your anger does not imply that you will never become furious or you bottle up this emotion. Instead, it entails learning to recognize, manage, and express anger in a healthy and constructive manner. Anger management is an accomplishment that can be cultured by everyone. There's always room for growth, even if you believe you've got your anger under control. Unmanaged anger usually leads to violent behavior, which you can learn to manage in this book. Anger management includes a number of ways to aid a person in coping with thoughts, feelings, and behaviors in a healthy and productive manner.

Anger is a positive force that can range from small irritation to fury. While many people think of rage as just a bad emotion, it may also be beneficial. I shall elaborate further on this later in the book, but angry sentiments may motivate you to stand up for someone or to affect societal change. On the other hand, anger may develop into violent action, such as screaming at someone or damaging property, if left unchecked. Anger may cause you to withdraw from your surroundings and turn your anger inwardly, which can have poor health and well-being repercussions. When anger is felt too frequently or powerfully, or when it is expressed in damaging ways, it becomes a problem. As a result, anger management techniques are useful and can assist you in finding appropriate methods to vent your emotions. Your emotions can be fuelled or inhibited by your beliefs and activities. So, if you want to change your emotional state from anger to happiness, you may change your thoughts and behaviors. Without fuel, the fire inside you will start to suffocate, and you will feel calmer. If you feel like your anger issues have affected your social and mental life, you have landed at the right place, and it is not time to act. You are going to learn valuable skills which you can employ to help manage your bad temperament. To find the root cause of the issue, you need to learn more about this emotion, identify what triggers it, and find an explanation for the differential expression of the same emotion between you and your husband, for example. You are going to learn about the different stages of anger, and although you may wonder how this is helpful, by the end of this, you are going to realize how important knowing this emotion is if you want to control it. You are going to understand why this emotion is important and how you can express it in a less negative way. There are small changes that you can make consistently whilst you put in the work routinely, like filling in anger management worksheets and incorporating music and exercise in your daily life. All of this and much more are featured in this workbook, and the information included in this book is an asset to the change you want to achieve.

Chapter 1:
What is Anger?

A nger isn't only the image of someone who is enraged to the point of being red in the face and shouting at the top of their lungs. It's a far more complex emotion than that. It manifests itself in minor ways, such as irritation or displeasure. It manifests itself in mild forms, like frustration when you're unable to achieve a goal you've been striving for. It also occurs in extremes, as seen by activities such as road rage. Anger, like joy, sorrow, worry, and contempt, is one of the most fundamental human emotions. These emotions have been perfected over the course of human history and are linked to fundamental survival. Anger is associated with the sympathetic nervous system's fight, flight, or freeze response, which prepares humans for confrontation. Fighting does not always include punches being launched. Anger is a negative emotion characterized by hatred against someone, or something you feel has intentionally upset you. It is commonly connected with stress, irritation, and anger. Anger is something that everyone encounters at some point in their lives. It's a very normal reaction to difficult or stressful circumstances. Anger becomes an issue only when it is shown excessively and begins to influence your everyday functioning and interpersonal relationships. Anger may range in intensity from mild irritation to outright wrath. It might be excessive or illogical at times. It may be difficult to keep your emotions under check in these situations, which may lead you to act in ways you wouldn't ordinarily.

Anger remains because it has certain benefits: it may inspire you to act, and it can help you gain what you want when others back down in a confrontation. Anger, on the other hand, has a number of expenses, which may be divided into three categories: physical, behavioral, and emotional. Physical Anger has been related to an increased risk of heart attacks, strokes, and irregular heartbeats after an outburst of rage. Behavioral refers to when you're upset; you're more likely to make risky decisions when driving or give up sooner when completing a tough activity. Anger takes many forms in different people, and people all exhibit it in different ways. Raised voices, clinched fists, tightened jaw, rapid heartbeats, and profuse perspiration are some of the external traits you may notice when you are angry. Anger is a perfectly natural and usually healthy emotion. When you lose control of it, though, it may be harmful to your emotional and physical health. Your body undergoes physiological and biochemical changes when you are furious. Your blood pressure and heart rate spike. Adrenaline and noradrenaline are two hormones that your body produces. Putting your body through these changes on a regular basis because of your anger can lead to medical problems and consequences, like developing hypertension, diabetes, insomnia, and bowel disorders, amongst others. Anger-induced stress chemicals can damage neurons in parts of the brain in charge of intuition and short-term recollection, as well as weaken the immune system. Your blood pressure, pulse, body temperature, and breathing rate may all rise as a result of these hormone releases, sometimes to potentially hazardous amounts. The 'fight or flight' reaction is a natural chemical reaction that is meant to just provide an immediate increase of energy and power. This suggests that the body and mind are getting ready for a battle or preparing to flee from danger. People who are frequently angry, on the other hand, are unable to successfully regulate their anger and can become unwell, much as unresolved stress might. Your bodies aren't built to deal with high amounts of adrenaline and cortisol for lengthy periods of time or on a frequent basis. Anger has the potential to be both productive and destructive. Anger or irritation, when well handled, has little negative health or interpersonal implications. Anger is, at its core, a signal that something in your surroundings isn't quite right. It grabs your attention and pushes you to do something about the problem. However, how you handle the anger signal has far-reaching implications for your general health and well-being. When you show anger, it causes others to feel defensive and furious as well, affecting your social circle too. Friends, co-workers, and family members get alienated as a result of out-of-control rage. It also has a strong link to health issues and early mortality. Anger that is hostile and violent raises your chance of dying young, as well as your risk of social isolation, which is a key risk factor for serious disease and mortality. These are just two of the many reasons why it's a good idea to learn how to control your anger.

People express anger in different ways; thus, it does not seem the same for everyone. Some people may express their fury via screams, but others may express their rage by physically hitting an object or even another person. Anger is a natural emotion, but it's important to learn how to express it in a healthy way, so you don't alienate others around you. It is also needed for your mental health to vent your anger in a healthy manner.

What has defined anger for you as a woman so far?

_____

_____

_____

_____

_____

_____

Is your definition of anger in line with the above explanation?

_____

_____

_____

_____

_____

_____

Describe one particular moment where you always find yourself getting angry?

_____

_____

_____

_____

_____

_____

_____

_____

_____

_____

_____

_____

_____

_____

_____

_____

Chapter 2:
How Is Anger Different in Men and in Women?

M en are more openly aggressive than women on average, so it's natural to believe that they're also angrier. This is not always the case. Women experience rage as frequently and as severely as males, according to research. Men who are furious are more prone to act aggressively, but this does not rule out the possibility that women are also driven by anger. The key difference might be that males felt less successful when pushed to manage their anger, whilst women tended to be better at controlling spontaneous anger reactions.

Some have speculated that the differences between men and women are due to variances in brain biology. While the amygdala is the same size in men and women, the orbital frontal cortex, which is engaged in moderating violent impulses, is substantially larger in women, according to research. They speculated that this might explain why women appear to be better at controlling violent outbursts. Additionally, there is substantial evidence that societal expectations play a role. It is well known that teachers treat girls and boys differently in school, which may have an impact on the capacity to manage these responses. Many women have been indoctrinated to feel that they must play the peacemaker to avoid upsetting others. They also consider harmony to be typical. Conflict is unnatural if peace is the norm. Women who publicly voice their anger with males are particularly questionable. Everyone is turned off by such enraged women, unlike heroes, who fight for what they believe in and even die for it. Women become unladylike, unfeminine, unmaternal, and sexually unappealing when they vent their anger directly toward males. Women's anger is typically shown in more subtle ways, such as passive-aggressive actions. A woman may become enraged indirectly rather than directly. On the surface, passive-aggressive action appears benign, yet behind the surface, anger surges. Women frequently employ nonverbals, particularly smiles, to reduce the impact of conflict and anger. She can't risk jeopardizing her femininity, and she feels compelled to get rid of her anger as quickly as possible. Women aren't meant to upset others; instead, they're supposed to be the master negotiator and mediators. So, while she may look kind, she is enraged. She avoids the turbulence of expressing and experiencing rage by being friendly. Allowing the productive expression of rage is one of the most difficult problems in conflict. It may be necessary to train or provide permission to women so that they may vent their rage without sacrificing their femininity or relationships, and this causes a build-up of unpleasant emotions.

While females are more prone than males to get angry for the same reasons, they deal with it differently. Men are more prone to express their rage through words or physical actions. Women, while increasingly doing the same, are far more likely to concentrate their rage inward. As a result, a highly self-critical internal discourse emerges, which may influence or contribute to sadness. Women are more inclined than males to redirect their rage. They may hide, externalize, or project their anger. You may have heard stories about how girls create an internal script that says women shouldn't be furious, that anger isn't feminine, and that it's wrong. Unfortunately, following these rules leads to inner unrest, which manifests as self-doubt, emotional avoidance, and disputes with others and oneself. Unfortunately, many women face a double standard in the workplace when it comes to anger. Men are given more flexibility in expressing their emotions, but women are frequently perceived as troublemakers when they do so. Another issue that women confront is that their anger may have less capacity to influence people than men's anger. Women are more likely than males to hang on to their anger due to the same causes that compel them to repress it. This is quite reasonable. Certain sentiments do not just vanish when you ignore, diminish, or reject them. They, on the other hand, demand your attention, particularly when they mirror internal pain. While males are given more leeway in expressing their anger, even to the point of hyper-masculinity, they are urged to sit with and accept the inner pain that underlies their rage. Women, on the other hand, are more inclined to sit with their pain rather than identify their rage owing to anger suppression.

There will be tension when there are relationships. There is tension in every job. When women aren't given effective dispute resolution skills, it can lead to costly issues, including low engagement, low morale, and poorly performing teams. Women can improve their conflict resolution skills and develop more constructive answers without jeopardizing their mental and social well-being. You owe it to our mothers, sisters, and daughters to help them recognize their anger while also finding appropriate outlets for it. Women can achieve this by increasing the amount of time they spend talking about anger and providing instruction on the various abilities that come with healthy anger. Through public policy, the courts, and the media, women can be supported and encouraged through the teaching of these skills in public schools, to parents, in the workplace, and in the media. Finally, women can gain if they commit to teaching the tools necessary to no longer be afraid of their anger and to be able to rely on their intelligence. Through healthy expression of anger, women can eliminate the stigma associated with anger management in women.

What are the things that enrage you as a woman?

_____

_____

_____

_____

_____

_____

_____

_____

Do these things enrage your male counterparts as well, your partner, your brother, or your father, perhaps?

_____

_____

_____

_____

_____

Do you believe your gender has an impact on how you handle your anger?

_____

_____

_____

_____

If you said yes above, explain how.

_____

_____

_____

_____

_____

_____

Chapter 3:
Signs You Have an Anger Issue

W hen it comes to anger issues, it's critical to recognize the warning signals and learn how to deal with them. This protects you against mental health issues, health problems, and relationship issues. The news and happenings in today's world may be overwhelming, confusing, and distressing. This might result in angry outbursts, which can negatively impact your quality of life. People experience fury from time to time, and it could even be beneficial; however, not everyone can keep their emotions in check. Uncontrolled anger isn't a pleasant sensation, especially when you must cope with the consequences. If this happens, you should think about whether you have an anger issue. Anger that is normal and anger that is a problem are two very different things. Unhealthy rage manifests itself in a variety of ways. Resentment, judgment, manipulation, and verbal or physical abuse are all examples of it.

So, how can you confirm whether you are struggling with anger management? And what can you do to get your anger under control? Check out these indicators that could help you figure out if you have a problem if you're not yet sure if your rage levels are normal or if they're getting out of hand.

- You are the passive-aggressive type- It's possible that people who are feeling passive rage are unaware that they are furious. Your emotions may manifest as sarcasm, indifference, or meanness while you are experiencing passive rage. You could engage in self-destructive habits like skipping work, alienating friends and family, or underperforming in professional or social situations. Outsiders will think you're deliberately undermining yourself, even if you don't understand it or can't justify your behavior. Acts like being rude or insulting to others, and giving them quiet treatment, are examples of passive-aggressive conduct.

- **Your outbursts of anger are above average-** Everyone gets furious, but not everyone hits walls, rages on the road, or verbally assaults others. If you reach this degree of anger, you clearly don't know how to regulate your emotions. Outbursts are common among those who have anger problems. Anger can become a mental health issue if it is accompanied by unexpected outbreaks of aggressiveness, impulsivity, or disruptive conduct. You are accidentally observed damaging stuff, abusing people, having regular aggressive driving, and having temper tantrums if you have anger issues. This has a bad impact on your skills, job, and personal relationships. It might also have repercussions. To cope successfully with this type of anger, you must learn to detect triggers and regulate angry symptoms.
- **Anger is displayed physically-** Anger has been portrayed as a negative emotion in culture in numerous ways. As a result, when an emotion occurs, people are at a loss as to how to express it. You may have noticed that you react to rage with physical actions on a regular basis. Physical responses to rage include rubbing your forehead, pacing, being sarcastic, wanting alcohol, and raising your voice. Shaking, sweating, an elevated heart rate, and shallow breathing are some of the physical reactions of rage. Shallow breathing is a recognizable symptom of anger for many people. Practice breathing techniques when you start to feel out of breath. Anger activates your body's fight-or-flight response, which releases adrenaline. You may relax your body by doing breathing exercises.
- **Your anger is disproportionate to the situation-** Outbursts aren't good, but neither is a protracted, simmering fit of rage or a total freakout that lasts forever. When rage persists for an extended period, it may indicate a problem. If your anger is not proportionate to the situation you are in, this may indicate an anger management issue.
- **Blaming others for how you are feeling-** It is always someone else's fault when something awful happens or goes wrong. Instead of taking onus for your own life, you place blame on others for what happens to you. Come back to this the next time

you want to point the finger at someone else for how you're feeling.

- You are constantly unhappy- Bitterness and despair are the opposites of happiness. Long-term sadness can be torturous not just for you but also for your loved ones. Because they find brief satisfaction or euphoria in detrimental activities like drug addiction, drinking, and smoking, some people turn to negative practices like these to overcome their sadness.

- You get irritated easily- Being irritated is a response to another person's wrongdoing or flaw. If you are unhappy or angry most times, you may get irritated by others even if what they are doing or saying should not make you feel that way. Controlling your emotions might be difficult if you're quickly agitated when conversing with someone who is bringing you anger problems. Find alternatives and disagree without being arrogant or dismissive of others. Even the smallest or petty things can make you angry if you struggle with managing your anger.

- You put yourself down- One of the symptoms that you have anger issues is resentment toward yourself. To handle this issue, you must first understand what causes this unpleasant emotion, as well as the source and severity of the emotion. Some people tend to hold inside anger more quietly, and it may not be obvious to others. Negative self-talk, self-loathing, and feelings of unworthiness are all examples of inward anger. Inward rage issues might manifest as that annoying nagging voice that tells you you're not good enough or continuously reminds you of your errors. People who are upset prefer to focus their thoughts on negative or negative occurrences while ignoring positive or positive ones.

- Difficulty expressing your emotions- Another typical reaction to anger is to get overly emotional. When you have an anger issue, you may find yourself quickly agitated, depressed, guilty, resentful, nervous, and wanting to leave the situation. It might be tough to express oneself in a calm and healthy manner when you are dealing with anger challenges. When it comes to reaching mutual agreements on controversial matters, this is often visible.

- You seek to be alone- When you don't express your anger in a healthy way, it might start to damage you inwardly, leading to feelings of isolation and self-harm. People who are depressed are more susceptible to these feelings and are more likely to act on their desire to harm themselves. Between avoiding confrontation and humiliation, you find yourself seeking to be alone most of the time. You find yourself ignoring people or refusing to socialize.

- You find yourself choosing alcohol or worse to escape your anger- Substances may quickly become a comfort for numbing angry sensations, leading to misuse and addiction. Without the assistance of a helpful drug and alcohol recovery program, this addiction may wreak havoc on one's life.

- You are surrounded by anger- Spending time with someone who is continuously yelling or in an angry mindset is unpleasant. Those who deal with anger issues frequently find themselves in harmful relationship patterns.

- You try to rationalize your angry behavior- You justify your actions by claiming that others around you are overly sensitive. The brain tries to justify the undesirable conduct at this moment.

- Anger seems the only way you can express yourself- You're having trouble expressing your feelings, so you're getting angry to take some control. You believe that your aggressive behavior might give you the upper hand over others. When you erupt in anger, you unintentionally hurt other people, and it looks like that is the exclusive you know how to express your emotions.

- Social media gets to you- While assertiveness can help you overcome fear and injustice when furious outbursts require you to react physically to news on TV or social media, this can indicate an anger problem. When dealing with this problem, it's critical to ground your self-talk and separate yourself from the source.

- Thinking of your past makes you uneasy- Your memory constantly brings up your past faults and failures. In such a situation, you'll probably be angry with yourself. Continuous resentment and aggravation toward specific situations and people might make you even angrier. Learn to forgive yourself when your baggage comes back to haunt you. To help you move ahead, spend some time recognizing the fundamental origins of your anger.

- Taking everything literally- People who are enraged frequently take things personally and are offended by them. They seek and anticipate criticism from others. Sometimes it's just not your fault. If someone is irritable and snappish with you, he or she may be having a rough day and not dealing with his or her anger properly. It's possible that it has nothing to do with you.

- Perfectionism- People who become furious frequently have unrealistic expectations of themselves or those around them. If these expectations are not realized, people feel betrayed and hurt. This pain develops into a rage.

- Fairness- The belief that there is an ultimate standard of good and wrong is the illusion of fairness. It assumes that there is a norm of fair behavior for all individuals and that all people will live up to those standards. What is reasonable for one individual may not be reasonable for another. What is fair is a completely subjective evaluation based on what each individual wants, needs, or expects in each scenario. Being fair would thus mean meeting each person's needs, whether they are similar or dissimilar to our own. Understanding that what is fair for you may not be for others and the other way round can be the first step towards reducing your anger.

- Self-fulfilling prophecy- Drawing negative inferences about life from isolated incidents and then viewing the world through those conclusions can lead to self-fulfilling prophecies. These are negative, cynical, and short-sighted assumptions that can become a reality.

While a certain amount of rage is acceptable and healthy, developing problems with anger management can be disastrous. Notice how you react to anger and follow this guide to help you manage your anger issue.

How many of the above do you relate to?

_____

_____

_____

_____

_____

_____

List them down below. Awareness is the key in this exercise! Unless you are aware of your behavior and what external factors affect your mood, you will not be able to make any changes.

_____

_____

_____

_____

_____

_____

_____

Chapter 4:
Types of Anger

Y ou're undoubtedly aware that individuals communicate their anger through a variety of communication strategies. Here is an overview of different anger styles to which you can relate yourself if you are a woman currently struggling to manage your anger:

The Aggressive style of anger- This is characterized by a strong need to maintain control over oneself, other people, and situations. They don't accept a negative answer and manipulate people by inflicting pain and or anger to make them feel bad or give in. Aggressive people generally utilize sarcasm, ridicule, put-downs, complaints, threats, and abuse to obtain what they want. This can also allude to the maladaptive anger type. You are dealing with a maladaptive emotional reaction when rage reaches frightening levels and impairs your judgment. Anger, if left unchecked, may lead to impulsive or defensive attitudes, which can have a severe influence on your personal and professional relationships. This has you making rushed judgments that you later come to regret. Irrational ideas, impatience, poor decision-making, impulsive behaviors, improper language, inflexible attitudes, and, in extreme cases, actual violence are all associated with maladaptive or dysfunctional types of anger. However, not everyone who is suffering from anger difficulties will express their feelings in a violent manner.

Passive anger- This is characterized by a desire to avoid conflict and confrontation. These people have a hard time saying no without feeling bad since they don't articulate their desires and feelings. Many people avoid admitting to being furious because they dislike confrontation. This manifests itself in behaviors such as becoming silent when angry, crying, postponing things, or avoiding them altogether and acting as if everything is Fine. Passive aggressiveness is motivated by a desire to be in command. This is also known as repressed aggressiveness. Those who repress negative feelings are on the other end of the spectrum. When confronted with events that elicit rage and unhappiness, they keep their sentiments locked up inside rather than expressing them.

Those who opt to repress anger, as opposed to those who express it through violence or passive-aggressive attitudes, are more prone to breaking. Repressed anger can lead to resentment, rumination, illogical beliefs, social isolation, gastrointestinal issues, high blood pressure, and sleeplessness, among other psychological and physiological repercussions.

The passive-aggressive style- Because it makes them feel bad, people with this style try hard to avoid hurting others. They also avoid enraging people to prevent feeling uneasy or afraid. People who have a Passive-Aggressive style are less outwardly aggressive toward others than those who have an aggressive anger style, but they also do not wish to avoid confrontation as much as those who have an aggressive anger type. Instead, when they're angry, they desire to punish themselves and may resort to seduction or deception to accomplish their goals. They are typically friendly to your face but employ behind-the-scenes tactics to get back at you. They may apply the silent treatment, withhold their love or attention, gossip, blow the whistle, or refuse to comply. When asked what's wrong, they frequently respond "nothing," even though their body language and actions blatantly indicate that something is wrong. People who are passive-aggressive exhibit their anger in subtle ways, which creates a stressful environment around them. If you're around a passive-aggressive individual, you'll undoubtedly notice that while things appear to be normal on the surface, something isn't quite right. Passive-aggressive people despise being told what to do, become uncooperative when someone or something gets in the way of their goals, take non-confrontational retribution, spread stories, and gossip, and exclude individuals from their peer group.

The projective-aggressive style- A person who adopts this style may look calm, yet this is not the case. They are frequently enraged and fear to own and express their rage. Instead, they project their rage onto others, and they may even persuade others to act out their rage on their behalf. They may accuse you of being angry when you are not.

The assertive anger style- People who have this anger style express their demands in a straightforward, upfront, and honest manner, rather than waiting for others to appreciate them. At the same time, they regard the needs and feelings of others. They hold themselves high up and expect others to do the same. They believe they oversee their own lives and decisions. Being in control and optimistic, communicating and listening, and being receptive and dealing with the problem are all ideal approaches to coping with anger. This assertive anger can aid in the progression of relationships. It will have you thinking before speaking and being confident in your delivery but remaining open and adaptable to the other party. It requires being patient without raising your voice, revealing your emotional condition, and genuinely seeking to understand what others are experiencing. When you deal with anger in this manner, you demonstrate maturity and concern for your relationships and yourself. This kind is also known as the adaptive rage type. Even though rage is an unpleasant and bad feeling, it may occasionally assist in navigating life's unforeseen difficulties. It's an emotional experience known as 'adaptive anger,' which mobilizes your internal resources and concentrates them on conquering barriers. When you find yourself abiding by regulations that you feel are not in your best interests, for example, anger leads people to protest. Anger serves two purposes in circumstances where your values, goals, and needs are at risk. On one side, it indicates a misalignment between your beliefs about what is best for you and what your environment has to offer. On the other side, it motivates people to seek out other options, demand fair treatment, and seek justice.

Constructive vs. destructive anger- It's a good idea to comprehend the distinction and figure out how to manage both in your life. Constructive rage may aid in healing, progress, and rehabilitation, but destructive anger can be harmful. Constructive rage may be studied or analyzed to help you better understand your circumstances, other people, and yourself. Furthermore, for anger to be productive and managed, a person must be conscious of it and acknowledge their own and others' needs. Here, your rage is being channeled to gain control of the situation and retain your self-respect. Destructive anger is expressed in an inappropriate manner that causes harm, such as lashing out violently by verbally or physically harming someone. It might be that the reaction is out of proportion when compared to the provocation. Anger may also be directed inside, culminating in intentional self-harm or substance abuse. It relieves tension in the short term, but it might have long-term detrimental implications. Destructive rage is common and powerful. These emotions might be even stronger. A person may be unconscious of their anger at times, or if they are aware, they may attempt to conceal or avoid it. When anger is not addressed, it tends to become stronger. The more intensive the emotion, the more likely it will be expressed in an unhealthy, perhaps dangerous manner.

Forgiveness is essential; if someone has apologized for making you upset, or if you realize the situation isn't worth the effort, be willing to forgive and ready to be forgiven as well as forgive yourself! This will assist you in de-stressing and enhancing your interpersonal interactions. Keep in mind that you are valuable. Your life matters and you have the power to make a difference in the world. You can learn ways to handle your aggression, relieving the stressful pressures brought by anger and its uncontrolled emotions.

What type of anger do you most relate to?

_____

_____

_____

_____

_____

_____

_____

_____

_____

Describe one particular incident in detail below where the above anger type was very evident. In this description, be sure to include what triggered this incident, who was involved, and your reaction.

_____

_____

_____

_____

_____

_____

_____

_____

_____

_____

_____

_____

_____

_____

_____

Chapter 5:
The Stages of Anger

A nger, like sorrow, fear, pleasure, and happiness, is an emotion that people experience. Anger is an active emotion that serves as a warning system when things aren't going well in your life. Anger is triggered by two factors: frustration is frequently induced by not obtaining what we want, especially if we were anticipating it, and by the belief that others do not respect or care about your feelings. It's quite easy to control your reaction to rage when it's only a little annoyance. Anger may become increasingly difficult to handle as it grows in intensity, depending on your experience and skill.

There are five stages to the anger cycle: trigger, escalation, crisis, recovery, and depression. Understanding the cycle allows you to better understand your own and others' emotions.

Trigger phase- When an incident sets off the anger cycle, this is known as the trigger phase. You get into a fight or learn something that disturbs you. At some level, you feel threatened, and your physiological system prepares to respond.

The escalation phase- This occurs when your body prepares for a crisis by increasing respiration through fastened breathing, increased heart rate, and blood pressure, tensing muscles for action, changing the pitch or volume of your voice, and changing the shape of your eyes, pupils widening, and lowering your eyebrows. Keep these indicators in mind the next time you get angry. Your body posture shifts as well.

The Crisis phase- The survival instinct, the fight or flight reaction, kicks in during this phase. Your body is ready for action. Unfortunately, your judgment quality is greatly diminished during this phase, and judgments may be made without the benefit of your finest reasoning skills. After some action has been taken during the crisis phase, the next phase begins.

The recovery phase- The body begins to recuperate from the high level of stress and energy expenditure during this phase. The amount of adrenaline in your blood decreases with time. As logic takes the role of the survival reaction, the quality of judgment returns.

The Post-Crisis or Depression Phase- This occurs when the body enters a brief phase in which the heart rate falls below normal for the body to rebuild its equilibrium.

These phases are all ticked in a situation where individuals are angry, whether they are kids in a classroom, employees at work, or couples in a relationship. Identifying the phases your body goes through during anger can help you keep an eye out for the triggers and for the signals your body sends to alert you of this strong emotion getting out of hand.

Chapter 6:
Facts About Anger

A nger is considered masculinity among males. Society frequently teaches people that it is inappropriate for women. However, cultural messaging that a woman's anger is toxic can have a harmful impact on a woman's mental and physical health. Being told that anger is a negative thing as a woman may lead to shame, which can prevent you from expressing this healthy emotion. While people have little control over how others react to your anger, understanding how to recognize, express, and regulate it may be liberating.

Here are some facts about anger that may change the way you view anger forever:

- Anger isn't a life-threatening feeling. Growing up in a family where conflict was either ignored or forcefully addressed might teach the attitude that anger is dangerous. It's critical to realize that rage does not do harm to people. What's harmful is how anger is expressed. Anger expressed by physical or verbal violence leaves emotional scars, but anger communicated non-violently can create connection and aid in relationship restoration.
- It indicates that we have been treated unfairly or have been injured in some manner. It might help you identify your needs and practice self-care if you don't feel embarrassed about your anger. Anger is the emotional red light.
- Hiding one's anger has repercussions. You can swallow your anger if you believe that anger is harmful. However, concealing this feeling has repercussions. Chronic anger has been connected to health issues such as sleeplessness, anxiety, and depression. Anger that remains unresolved and unspoken can lead to undesirable habits such as substance abuse, overeating, and overspending. Uncomfortable emotions need to be calmed, and if you don't receive loving support, you must find other methods to cope.

- Expressing your feelings is what keeps them healthy. Even if confronting the harmful person or scenario feels hazardous, cathartic outlets for anger can be found in journaling, music, meditation, or talking with a therapist. A lot of user-friendly solutions are going to be featured in the coming pages.

- Anger that is linked to a specific outcome might be emotionally dangerous. If the person or circumstance does not change, relying on your anger to influence results might leave you feeling helpless, unhappy, and disappointed. With that in mind, ask yourself, "What do I want to gain from this communication?" and "How will I feel if nothing shifts?" before questioning someone. You can't alter other people, which can be frustrating, but it can also be liberating to understand what you can and can't manage.

- Anger may be expressed in a healthy way. One of the most effective methods to communicate anger orally is to use "I" phrases. Owning your feelings might help the other person hear and accept your remarks by softening their barriers. Instead of stating, "You constantly irritate me," say, "I'm irritated because..."

- If confronting the individual isn't an option, channeling your passion into activism may create a supportive and therapeutic feeling of community.

- Knowing that your experience may benefit another person can feel empowering in cases when individuals have endured trauma such as abuse, assault, or the death of a loved one.

- The term "changing your mind" has taken on a whole new meaning because of science. Neuroplasticity: What precisely does that entail? The brain's capacity to alter its shape and function over time is known as neuroplasticity. Behavioral patterns and anatomical structures in the brain can change with exercise. Certain parts of the brain used on a regular basis might thicken and grow. When it comes to anger management, rage-inducing circumstances should end in reasonable thought and constructive conduct.

I hope that by the beginning of this chapter, you simply thought that anger was a negative emotion that seemed difficult to control but ended this chapter by reconsidering your impression of anger. Like you should keep experiencing happiness, you should also keep experiencing anger as this is not an emotion to be avoided. The goal is to learn how to control and express it in a positive and beneficial manner.

Chapter 7:
Why Should You Learn to Control Your Anger?

A re you aware that learning to control your anger is beneficial to your health? People who control their anger are less likely to get sick and are happier emotionally. Even while anger is a natural emotion, it may occasionally lead to unsettling or out-of-control actions. You can even believe that your anger is overpowering you. There are a variety of reasons why people struggle to control their anger and aggressive behaviors. The causes are exhibited differently from person to person, and a mix of elements come into play too. Perhaps you've been taught that expressing rage is not pleasant or inappropriate. Perhaps you've witnessed excessive anger and violence at home, in your community, or at school, which has distorted your perception of your experience with anger. It's also possible that you're having trouble controlling your rage because you haven't yet learned how to deal with the feelings you're experiencing. Having trouble understanding and regulating anger, even at a young age, increases your risk of developing health problems down the line Because your mind and body are linked. Not dealing with angry emotions puts your body under stress, which can lead to physical issues.

Anger management issues might also raise your likelihood of getting mental health issues. Teenagers who struggle to control their anger have fewer friends, have more behavioral issues and get poorer marks in school. This is because, even if they receive a lot of attention for their aggressive actions, kids who struggle with anger are frequently miserable and alone. These patterns do not only happen to kids and teenagers but to adults too. When you're becoming too angry, your body has multiple strategies of letting you know, like increased heart rate, tightened muscles, and heavier breathing. Even the most serene individuals can become enraged at times. It is healthy to get angry on occasion, for example, when injustice occurs or when someone's rights are violated. As a result, it is an unavoidable aspect of existence. Anger management skills will assist you in identifying the source of your rage and expressing it in a healthier manner. You will be able to communicate your point more clearly because of this. Many have developed habits to assist them in coping with intense emotions. Unlearning inefficient coping strategies and relearning more constructive methods to deal with the difficulties and frustrations that lead to anger is part of anger management.

Anger only becomes an issue when it spirals out of control and causes harm to you or others. This might happen if you consistently express your anger in unhelpful or harmful ways or if your anger is negatively affecting your mental and physical health. When anger becomes your default feeling, cutting off your capacity to feel other emotions, or when you haven't found healthy ways to express your anger, you should learn to regulate it. How you react when you're angry is determined by your ability to recognize and manage your emotions, as well as how you've learned to express them. Ignoring or refusing to speak to people, refusing to complete duties, or purposefully doing things incorrectly are all bad ways to deal with anger. It is not the correct approach to deal with rage to persuade yourself that you blame yourself and deny yourself your fundamental necessities. Screaming, cursing, slamming doors, punching or throwing things, and being physically or verbally abusive and threatening to others are not healthy ways to deal with anger. If you find yourself expressing your anger through external aggressiveness and hostility, it may be scary and harmful to others around you, particularly children. And it may have huge implications: you could lose your family, your career, and run afoul of the law. Even if you're never physically violent or aggressive toward others, or even if you never raise your voice, you may recognize some of these angry behaviors and believe they're an issue for you.

Whatever the cause, the next stage is to learn how to recognize what makes you angry and how to control your actions, even when your anger is legitimate. Anger management is a concept that refers to the abilities required to recognize when you or someone else is growing angry and then take appropriate action to resolve the problem in a good manner. It does not imply that you should internalize or conceal your anger, but rather that you should recognize the causes and indicators of anger and find alternative, more acceptable methods to express yourself.

Chapter 8:
Anger at the Workplace

Y ou're upset because you were passed over for another major promotion? Angry that the same people constantly manage to get ahead in your company? Perhaps it's time to think about if your anger, however, justified, is holding you back. Evidence reveals that many of us are resentful at work, even though we may be uninformed of the long-term consequences of our behavior on our careers and co-workers. Workplace rage may create major health problems, such as persistent anxiety, depression, high blood pressure, and heart disease, in addition to being potentially destructive to the business. Learning to manage your anger in a positive way will enhance your health and make you a more valuable and promotable employee. Anger can sometimes come from outside sources. Employees are frequently coping with difficult circumstances in their personal life, and their anger might spill over into the workplace. Divorce, family loss, financial stress, and severe diseases may all make a person feel overwhelmed and irritable. People are hardly taught how to cope with loss and difficult events, so most prefer to hide their feelings, which might eventually manifest as anger or rage.

Everyone has been angry at work at some point: you do an all-nighter on a project that is subsequently scrapped, a customer criticizes your team for no apparent reason, or a co-worker shows up late for an important presentation, dumping all the preparation on you. These annoyances at work may make your blood boil. Your attention is instantly diverted away from the critical work at hand. Instead, your mind switches to fight-or-flight mode, and you become reactive, incapable of thinking rationally, blaming others, or reprimanding yourself for being furious. You're more likely to make terrible decisions and say things you'll later regret if you're in this mindset. In the workplace, it's totally acceptable to feel a variety of emotions, including anger. Negative emotions are sure to arise at work, just as they are in our personal lives, and this isn't always a negative thing. Learning to effectively communicate your emotions is essential for increasing your emotional intelligence, which may help you become a more successful leader. In fact, feeling enraged might help you focus and inspire you to handle the situation at hand. Learning to channel your frustration and obtain what you want in a constructive, professional manner will help you channel your frustration and achieve what you want without giving you a reputation as the office bully.

You may feel disconnected in your daily job tasks as well as your long-term career with so much turbulence in the workplace these days. It's difficult to retain your cool when insecurity leads to irritation. When you're in a leadership position, though, you're faced with an even greater challenge: controlling your team's moods without allowing their outbursts to undermine your performance. In the workplace, rage and losing one's cool are nothing new. According to several studies, job stress is by far the major source of stress in one's life. However, working through the pandemic, worries about racial justice, and higher turnover have all been particularly frustrating aspects for employees and executives in recent years. If you are a woman in charge of a team at work, controlling such emotions can be an even bigger challenge. You are responsible for keeping everyone happy all the time as the leader of your team, but you are in charge of creating a culture of trust and psychological safety.

As obvious as some of these may seem, here are some reasons why employees may feel angry at work:

- Employees are promised a raise, a promotion, or a major project, but it never materializes.
- An employee is directed to execute something he believes is inappropriate or wrong.
- The employee fails to meet a supervisor's expectations because the standards are too high, constantly changing, or there is insufficient training.
- The supervisor is a micromanager who regularly criticizes the employee.
- The employee believes that they are more qualified and talented than their boss.
- A co-worker who does the same job makes more money.

35

Here are some ways how to control and manage anger at the workplace:

- When people are angry, they are prone to justifying, blaming others, or urgently attempting to calm themselves down. Rather than going to rationalization, realize that the anger is valid and natural. Anger is profoundly ingrained in the genetic makeup. It's how you protect yourself against risks and threats to your health. The next time you feel yourself becoming furious, remember that avoiding it will not help. Instead, find a healthy, self-respecting technique to vent or disarm your anger. Rather than resisting your emotion, accept it.
- If you're going to lose your cool, the first thing you should do is find a method to break the habitual thought cycle that's been set in motion. Disconnecting physically from the situation can help: Take a stroll, leave your desk to make a phone call, or take a few deep breaths. Another strategy that might help you manage anger in the long run, is to practice visualizations. Consider how you feel while you're reacting to your rage. Imagine controlling your rage and dealing with the matter in a calm, constructive manner. You have a higher chance of managing your anger constructively and not allowing it to overwhelm you if you approach it with mindfulness.
- To avoid a full-fledged meltdown, you must first understand who and what gets you upset. When you're furious, pay attention to the situations and people around you so you can better predict and regulate your emotions in the future. Nobody likes being furious, so keep cool and collected by anticipating triggering events.
- When you decide to tackle the issue that is making you furious, make sure you have spent time understanding and articulating your sentiments beforehand. Emotional labeling is crucial because it may help you communicate your thoughts, opinions, and wishes more clearly. Speak to your supervisor or whoever is bothering you in the way you want to be communicated with.
- While it's tempting to linger on what is making you angry, and it may feel comforting at first, doing so won't help you in the long term. Ruminating is harmful because it diverts time and

mental resources away from problem-solving and keeps you locked in a bad emotional state. Instead, concentrate on the lessons you can take away from the scenario so that you may go on in a positive manner.

- It's normal for your sentiments to be influenced by those of your teammates. However, you must first regulate your temperament before reacting rashly to their anger. If you sympathize with their problems but don't know how to address them, you may begin to dodge when difficulties arise, showing attention but then changing the subject and doing nothing. And, if you're already emotionally distanced from your teammates, your initial reaction may be defensiveness as a means of self-preservation.

- Depersonalize how you respond to direct and indirect anger feedback from your team. It's critical to think of these inputs as data rather than a threat. You'll get an opportunity to express yourself later, but for now, don't get caught up in how your team's rage affects you. Remember that anything your team is going through, whether you sympathize with them or not, provides you with essential information for your leadership role if you hold one.

- You may start using strategies to help them channel their rage into more favorable outcomes. Helping your team manage and shift their emotions not only makes everyone feel better but may also generate greater inspiration in terms of what improvements to make and how to begin. You may also use their anger to help them build more stamina and resilience in their performance by creating goals and expectations in a certain way. You may turn anger into a good and constructive feeling by co-creating objectives with your team that enhances their potential and set them up for success.

- Consider whether your leadership style has any blind spots that might be contributing to their rage. Given the numerous concerns that are causing the employee to get angry these days, it's probable that you aren't the primary cause of your team's dissatisfaction. However, how you interact with them as a company and personally as their leader may either create conflict or build trust.

- Control your bodily reaction to rage by doing things like exercising, getting adequate sleep, and staying away from alcohol. You are more likely to respond correctly to situations if you are in good health.

As much as possible, stay away from anger. This is not to say that you should conceal your emotions, but rather that you should enhance your view of yourself and life so that you are less likely to become irritated. Anger is an emotion you'll face throughout your work and will need to learn to handle if you want to be a leader. The goal is to make sure you have the tools you need to deal with and articulate your anger successfully, professionally, and in a way that will benefit your career in the long run. Anger among your team members may exacerbate a demanding leadership position. However, how you handle your employees' complaints is crucial to ensure that negative emotions don't restrict your productivity. You can not only restrain their frustration by following these tips, but you can also use them to gain more trust and incentive for future performance.

Describe some of the most common moments (at least three) where you find yourself enraged at work.

_____

_____

_____

_____

_____

_____

From the above moments you have described, is there a way these moments can be completely avoided, or do you have no control over what triggers your anger?

Moment 1.	*I have no control*	*It can be avoided*
Moment 2.	*I have no control*	*It can be avoided*
Moment 3.	*I have no control*	*It can be avoided*

From the suggested ways to handle anger at work, choose three of the proposed solutions above that you will most likely use the next time you get angry at work.

_____

_____

_____

_____

_____

_____

_____

_____

_____

Chapter 9:
Anger in a Relationship

T hose who have been or are in a relationship understand how difficult it can be. Every relationship is made up of selfish people who have varying expectations. If you expect perfection all the time, you will be dissatisfied at some point. It's quite common for couples to experience arguments in their relationships. And while many couples recognize that they will not always agree, they do not see the dangers of rage in their relationship. Anger is the emotion that people experience while they are experiencing negative thoughts. Anger isn't always a terrible thing. However, the method in which individuals frequently display their anger is harmful.

When anger is not managed appropriately in a relationship, it can lead to irreversible consequences. It's also simple to become enraged when someone else is enraged with you. That implies the disagreement can continue to rise until you are yelling at each other or have taken the other approach and opted to ignore each other entirely. When neither party can maintain their composure, a little argument might quickly escalate into a major one. It also expands the scope of the debate beyond what it was initially about. When anger isn't managed properly, it can lead to verbal, emotional, or physical violence. In a relationship, no type of abuse is acceptable. Name-calling, demeaning, striking, or causing physical harm are all examples of this. Anger in a relationship isn't always a bad thing. In fact, unaddressed anger issues can result in some of the most prevalent relationship difficulties. However, if you're having trouble controlling your anger, especially when it comes to how you react to your partner, understanding how to control anger in a relationship might just save your relationship. You must remember that not all anger is negative. There are times and places when expressing rage is appropriate and warranted. Healthy anger may be a safety precaution to warn you of a hazardous circumstance. It might even be the result of seeing things in your relationship that aren't quite right. Anger troubles in relationships may arise because of something you've been resentful about for a long time. The key to establishing whether

40

your rage is legitimate is to find out whether it arises from a lack of understanding by your spouse or is a reaction to something that happened outside the relationship, such as a previous conversation with a family member. It might be an issue if you take your frustrations out on your spouse, and they have no influence over why you're unhappy. In a relationship, passion should not imply that emotions like anger are exhibited in irrational ways. Managing anger and your response to an infuriated spouse is a crucial ability that may help any love relationship grow in connection and maturity.

Here are some common anger triggers in a relationship:

- Being around someone who isn't respectful might be challenging. If your spouse continues to upset you despite your repeated attempts to communicate your feelings, you may experience an angry outburst.
- A companion who is often late might be frustrating, especially if you are a punctual person.
- You may be having difficulties if you believe your spouse does not prioritize you or if they seem to place everything and everyone else before you. It might be difficult to contain your anger in a relationship where you don't feel valued, but it is achievable.
- It's annoying to feel like your partner is always putting work ahead of you.
- Being financially responsible is an important part of being an adult. It's easy to become enraged and resentful when you're in a relationship with someone who doesn't share that responsibility.
- It might be discouraging to feel like you're not on the same page or that your goals aren't aligned. It might be so aggravating that you may get enraged each time it occurs.
- Being in the company of someone with a good sense of humor may be a real treat. It may also be irritating if one relationship partner responds to serious issues with humor.

- If your spouse has grudges against you for things you've done or said in the past and you believe you'll never be forgiven, it might lead to anger.

Here are some clues to help manage your anger with your loving partner:

- Learning to wait a minute or two before responding and taking a big breath may do wonders for your relationship. If you're having trouble restoring your calm, try counting to ten. Couples can benefit from this activity as a means of communication. With enough effort, you'll eventually be able to let go of your anger and react calmly, which can be more productive and conducive to reaching a common ground.
- You should be able to determine what you're truly experiencing after taking a few moments to calm down and examine the issue. Explain why you're unhappy with your lover in a calm manner. Anyone can Be straightforward and assertive but resist the need to be aggressive. If you're upset because your spouse was late for dinner again, use "I" phrases to express your feelings rather than blame them directly since they may respond with defense, and the conflict may escalate.
- Anger may drive people to become more theatrical and unreasonable, as well as say things they don't mean. You may re-create how we react to circumstances by focusing on how you react and avoiding terms like "always" and "never." Cognitive restructuring, also known as cognitive reframing, is a cognitive-behavioral method that aids in the transformation of negative emotions into more positive ones.
- A couple's therapist can assist you and your spouse in identifying the source of your relationship's anger. Therapists can also assist you in figuring out how to deal with anger in conflicts or when your other half does something that irritates you. This way, you and your spouse may work together to improve your relationship and reduce the likelihood of angry outbursts.

- There will be occasions when you are really enraged. It's possible that you'll require more than a minute. A deep breath might not be enough. It is just as important to know when to walk away as it is to understand what makes you angry. If you need to, physically leaving the area or location you're in may allow you enough time to collect your thoughts and let go of your anger before re-entering the situation.

- Anger may sometimes make things worse than they need to be. Humour is an excellent method and tactic for defusing tense circumstances. If you can utilize the first advice to take a breath and pause for a beat, you might be able to extract something humorous from the scenario and react to that rather than your anger. In some instances, humor is inappropriate, so be aware of how your spouse is feeling and tread carefully.

- If you can't let go of your own anger, you might want to work on being able to forgive, just as your partner's grudge might be an anger trigger for you. Positive and healthy emotions may be easily pushed out by negativity. If you're feeling overwhelmed by your anger, consider forgiving your spouse for whatever it is that has offended you. Forgiveness has a lot of power. It implies that you can let go, and part of what you're letting go of might be some unresolved anger issues. A genuine discussion with your spouse can assist you in resolving conflicts and learning to let go.

- Exercise has long been known and shown to relieve stress, which can lead to anger. Getting your heart rate up by going for a walk, run, or bike ride can help you eliminate yourself from the chaos, especially if you're going through a difficult period in your relationship.

- Going silent may briefly relieve your stress, but it is likely to exacerbate your partner's uneasiness or anger. This is not to say that you must sit down and address an issue right now. Rather than walking away, explain to your spouse that you need some time to calm down and gather your thoughts. Let them know that working out the differences is essential to you and that you'll think about how much time you need to consider before returning to them.

- If your partner gives you the silent treatment because you missed an anniversary, you've felt anxious about what may happen next. You cannot make someone talk to you, but you can let them know that you're willing to share your ideas and collaborate when they're ready. Attempting to compel or force them into a rapid reconciliation would almost certainly backfire, causing them to shut off even more.

- When someone you care about is distressed with you, you typically feel driven to placate and calm them down as soon as possible. However, you can't control anybody else's ideas, behaviors, or emotions; you are only responsible for your own. Being calm is much more successful than attempting to calm someone else, and individuals who can stay focused on regulating their own emotions and responses allow the other person in the room to do the same.

- When you're angry or irritated with a spouse, venting to a friend, your child, or even your therapist might be soothing. An emotional triangle occurs when we employ a third person to control our concern over another individual. It is very natural to want to vent, and it is not a bad thing. However, sometimes this prevents people from resolving the issue in the first place, and it can make your spouse feel lonely or even defensive. So, the next time you're angry with your spouse and want to call someone, think about if you're discussing this incident to find someone who agrees with you. While there's nothing wrong with telling your therapist about your relationship problems, keep in mind that it's their duty to be objective and help you think clearly, not to agree with you that your spouse is the bad one.

- Certain issues are more likely to elicit an angry or nervous emotion, which might result in conflict. Money, politics, religion, sex, parenting, and family dysfunction are frequently discussed. It's tempting to believe that having opposing viewpoints might lead to resentment and conflict, but your

44

uncontrolled reactions to these matters, rather than our actual viewpoints, are more often to blame. So, instead of focusing on settling disputes as swiftly as possible, return your attention to replying as maturely as possible. This isn't to say you must put up with a partner's violence or even that you must stay in a relationship. Maturity is defined as the ability to control one's emotions rather than allowing them to rule the show.

Anger may be a positive feeling, but when it becomes a problem in your relationship or in your life, you must learn to manage it. Getting your emotions under control is one of the best things you can do, whether it's learning how to regulate jealousy and anger in a relationship or any other sensation that's coming between you and your spouse. Nobody loves those who continually and unpredictably lash out at others around them. Anger is also dangerous for your emotions if you are always angry. Taking control of your anger is an important first step *toward better health and relationships.*

What does your partner do that triggers your anger?

_____

_____

_____

_____

_____

_____

_____

_____

Is your partner aware of your temperament and how their behavior affects you?

_____

_____

_____

_____

_____

What solutions can you utilize from the above list that will help lessen these moments of anger between you and your partner? List them below

_____

_____

_____

_____

_____

_____

_____

_____

Chapter 10:
Underlying Medical Conditions for Anger

A nger is induced by a variety of factors, including stress, family problems, and financial concerns. Anger in certain people can be caused by underlying medical conditions such as alcoholism and depression. Anger is not considered a problem in itself, but it is a documented sign of various mental health problems. Anger is an expression of deeper emotions. You are never furious until you are going through something deeper. Anger stems from fear, whether conscious or unconscious. Anger stems from pain, a wound tearing into you that you can't help but respond to. Anger is fuelled by pain, by the prolonged, often intense, and frequently excruciating agony. It is up to the person to understand the causes of their rage and do their best to discover a positive way ahead based on that understanding. However, as part of that constitution, it is also the individual's responsibility to recognize how they may lead others to experience fear, hurt, or suffering. Anger is attempting to communicate with us. Right now, there is a lot of rage on the planet. There is a lack of understanding of the actual fear, hurt, and sorrow that others are experiencing. People are reacting to anger as if it were fundamental rather than the emotions that underlie it. And that lack of comprehension feeds greater rage by inflicting more harm.

People may address the fundamental reasons for anger more successfully if they understand its roots - that is, the basic emotions that drive it. This is a critical first step in dealing with anger management issues. Most individuals find it difficult to experience fear and grief because it makes them feel vulnerable and out of control. As a result, people try to escape unpleasant sensations in any manner they can. One method is to subconsciously go into rage mode. Unlike fear and sadness, rage may bring a burst of energy and make you feel more in control, as opposed to helpless or powerless. In essence, rage may be used to gain control and authority in the face of vulnerability and uncertainty. When a partner gets angry, the fear of being abandoned often lurks beneath the surface. In these cases, anger can be fueled by a mixture of fear and imminent loss. Uncertainties that arise when ignorance dominates and things look ambiguous can also lead to anger. Uncertainty is associated with the unknown, which most people find frightening. Boredom, on the other hand, can elicit rage or annoyance because it can be coupled with a slight sensation of loss or anxiety related to the experience of not participating in something interesting or constructive. While having some sense of control is associated with improved emotional well-being, having an overwhelming need for control only leads to misery because it is impossible to constantly be in control, particularly of other people's actions. Anger is frequently characterized as a protective emotion since it activates your flight or fight reaction in response to a perceived external danger. However, other emotions must be sensed in order for anger to be aroused. These feelings are frequently the underlying reasons for anger, although they might be difficult to see if you are blinded by your anger.

Here are some underlying medical conditions that contribute to an anger management problem:

Perimenopausal Anger

Perimenopause is the phase before menopause. It happens when your ovaries progressively start producing less estrogen. Because your body's hormonal balance is shifting, it's common to encounter symptoms such as hot flashes and night sweats. You may also experience a slowdown in your metabolism. Menopause's hormonal changes, paired with its side effects, can have a substantial influence on your mood. It's not uncommon to have mood swings, despair, or even anger during this period. In fact, according to some research, irritation is the most prevalent symptom for 70% of women going through this phase. These changes usually begin in your mid-40s and might linger for a few months to many years. You've entered clinical menopause when you've gone a year without having a monthly period. Perimenopausal anger may feel very different from your regular anger or annoyance. In a matter of minutes, you might shift from feeling stable to feeling deeply bitter or angered. Your relatives and friends may also notice that you are less patient than normal. Some doctors believe that if you have had severe premenstrual symptoms your whole life, you are more prone to develop severe perimenopause mood swings. If this describes you, you should be on the lookout for other perimenopausal symptoms such as irregular bleeding, reduced sex drive, insomnia, and vaginal dryness. Consult your healthcare practitioner if you are having any of these symptoms. They can confirm your diagnosis and provide a treatment plan to help you feel better. Your perimenopausal anger does not indicate that you are insane. You won't feel like this forever. What you're feeling is due to a chemical reaction. Estrogen influences serotonin production. Serotonin is a mood stabilizer and happiness enhancer. When your body generates less estrogen, your emotions may go out of control. After your body adjusts to the drop in estrogen, your emotions should normalize.

It's possible that your anger will come and go. It may be more visible for a week or two before disappearing for the next month or so. This is caused by your decreasing estrogen levels. With each period of decrease, your estrogen-serotonin balance will be thrown off. You may take actions to help balance your hormones and recover control of your moods. It may become simpler to comprehend and live with this symptom after you make space in your thoughts to recognize and resolve your anger. You might wish to keep your rage to yourself so that it doesn't bother anyone else. However, research shows that self-silencing, or finding strategies to avoid recognizing and expressing your anger, increases your chances of developing depression. Listen to your body and realize that what you're feeling might be due to your body's adjustment. Some lifestyle choices, such as excessive coffee use and cigarette smoking, can cause anxiety. Dehydration might also increase your susceptibility to mood swings. And if your sleep is regularly disrupted by menopausal symptoms, you may find it difficult to deal with difficult emotions. However, everyone's body functions differently. Keep a daily notebook for at least two weeks to try to identify these triggers. You should keep track of what you ate, how much sleep you received if you exercised, and how you felt during the day. If journaling isn't your style, mood tracking or period forecasting apps are excellent alternatives. When you are in the heat of an argument, take a step back to consider where your feelings are coming from. Don't berate yourself for being angry; instead, address the source of your resentment. "Would I be so upset if I was feeling better?" you could ask yourself. You'll be better equipped to deal with anger if you're aware that you're prone to escalate emotions right now. Mind-body treatments, such as meditation and yoga, have been shown to assist perimenopausal women. Deep breathing methods and other mindfulness activities can help you sleep better and reduce the number of menopausal symptoms that keep you up at night. You may begin to incorporate these practices into your life by downloading a mindfulness app for your phone or enrolling in yoga classes to learn the fundamentals. Finding a way to express yourself may aid in the reduction of mood swings. Cardio, for example, can help protect you from gaining weight when your metabolism slows. Exercise also increases the supply of serotonin, which is required to raise and maintain your emotions. Gardening, painting, or sculpting, for example, might help you focus on building a quiet place in your mind to work through your emotions and find space for yourself.

Speak with your healthcare practitioner if you believe medication may be beneficial. They can show you your options and assist you in finding something that meets your specific requirements. Counseling and anger management are methods that can assist you in controlling your anger. Researchers discovered that women with diabetes and menopausal symptoms benefited considerably from group therapy that emphasized self-care. Seek advice from your healthcare provider to see if there are any support groups, anger management classes, or a counselor that specializes in perimenopausal anger. Talk to your healthcare physician if you already feel like your anger is interfering with your ability to accomplish your work or function in your relationships. Though some individuals assume differently, constantly feeling angry or unhappy during perimenopause is not normal. Your healthcare practitioner can help you in identifying and comprehending your symptoms, as well as developing a treatment strategy.

Intermittent Explosive Disorder

Intermittent explosive disorder (IED) is an often-misdiagnosed mental condition characterized by periods of rage and abrupt outbursts in which the person loses control completely. This mental disorder generally manifests itself throughout childhood or adolescence. Most people, however, continue to feel it later in life. Intermittent explosive disorder treatment may differ from person to person, but the typical treatment techniques include psychotherapy and medication. The intermittent explosive disorder causes you to be angry and violent for no apparent reason. It consists of a succession of verbal outbursts, physical battles, and eruptions of rage. Some symptoms might assist you in determining your problem. People with this illness are prone to throwing or breaking items, abusing people, and displaying road rage. This conduct stresses you out and has an impact on your daily activities and relationships. In most circumstances, it can also result in financial and legal consequences. It is a chronic condition that normally improves with age. Several environmental and genetic variables may have a role in the development of this illness. Some of the recognized causes of the intermittent explosive disorder include family history, verbal or physical abuse as a teenager, Brain function and chemistry, particularly fluctuating serotonin levels, Long-term trauma, ADHD, antisocial personality disorder, borderline personality disorder, depression, anxiety-related symptoms, or substance-abuse disorder as examples of mental health illnesses. An episode of the intermittent explosive disorder can occur at any moment. Some persons suffer episodes on a regular basis, while others remain nonaggressive for weeks or months at a time. An average occurrence lasts less than 30 minutes. The severity of symptoms varies among IED patients. Some people may feel less inclined to be verbally abusive, but they may exhibit strong physical hostility. Symptoms of the intermittent explosive disorder include anger, frustration, and irritability. Among the symptoms include irritability with human contact, scattered thinking, high activity levels, and chest tightness—people suffering from intermittent explosive disorder act impulsively. Most of them subsequently come to regret their actions. To help identify the illness, doctors frequently use the standard Psychiatric Diagnostic Manual. It states that to be diagnosed, a person must have three incidents of IED at any point in their lives. These episodes should not be the result of any external or internal influence. The individual must also exhibit bodily signs, such as injuring someone or causing property damage. If you have had similar instances, see your doctor for a proper diagnosis. Psychotherapy is the most effective treatment for the intermittent explosive disorder. Some doctors may recommend drugs in addition to therapy. Cognitive-behavioral therapy assists patients with IEDs in gaining control of and changing their habits. It might assist you in identifying the sources of your violent reactions. Relaxation methods and cognitive skills can help you manage and regulate your aggressive behavior and improve your communication and problem-solving abilities. Antidepressants such as serotonin reuptake inhibitors (SSRIs) and anticonvulsants may aid in mood stabilization. Other medications may be prescribed by your doctor. People who have IEDs frequently have little control over themselves. Professional treatment, on the other hand, can help you regulate your anger. You can't make a change until you restructure your thinking; therefore, attempt to discover logical reasoning in an aggressive scenario and react logically to it. Never skip a treatment session or any medicine given by your doctor. Even if you believe you do not require it, see your doctor before making any decisions on your own. Before reacting rashly, try to listen to the other person's reasoning. Incorporate breathing exercises into your daily routine and meditate on a regular basis. Following a certain routine might lead to dissatisfaction, so develop a timetable for your day and incorporate diverse interests into it. The effects of alcohol and recreational substances on your mood are substantial. Try to avoid them altogether.

Depression

Anger can be indicative of depression, which is defined as persistent sorrow and loss of interest that lasts at least two weeks. Anger can be restrained or expressed openly. The level of the anger and the way it is conveyed differs from person to person. You may also have additional symptoms if you have depression. These include impatience, fatigue, feelings of hopelessness, and suicidal or self-harming ideas.

Obsessive-Compulsive Disorder

Obsessive-compulsive disorder (OCD) can be classified as a kind of anxiety illness marked by obsessive thoughts and compulsive activity. A person with OCD has unwelcome, unsettling ideas, desires, or visions that cause them to do something again and over again. For example, people may do specific routines, such as counting to a number or repeating a word or phrase, because they have an illogical fear that if they don't, something horrible will happen. Anger has been identified as a prevalent symptom of OCD in studies. It affects almost half of all OCD sufferers. Anger may arise as a consequence of irritation with your inability to control obsessive thoughts and compulsive activities or as a result of someone or something interfering with your capacity to perform a ritual.

Attention Deficit Hyperactivity Disorder

ADHD is a neurodevelopmental disorder often characterized by symptoms such as inattention, hyperactivity, or impulsivity. Symptoms usually appear in early childhood and persist throughout a person's life. Some people are not diagnosed with this until they are adults, which is frequently referred to as adult ADHD. Anger and irritability can develop in persons of all ages with ADHD. Other symptoms include agitation, difficulty concentrating, poor time management, and poor planning abilities.

Oppositional defiant disorder

Oppositional defiant disorder (ODD) is a behavioral condition that affects 1 to 16% of school-aged children. Anger, impatience, and a quick temper are all common indicators of ODD. Children with ODD are frequently irritated by others. They may be rebellious and abrasive.

Bipolar Disorder

Bipolar disorder is a neurological illness that causes extreme mood swings. These strong mood swings can range from mania to sadness; however, depression does not affect everyone with bipolar illness. Many patients with bipolar illness have episodes of fury, impatience, and anger. You may get easily agitated, feel euphoric, have racing thoughts, and engage in impulsive or reckless conduct during a manic episode. During a depressed episode, you may feel sad, hopeless, or emotional, lose interest in previously cherished activities, and consider suicide.

Grief

One of the phases of grieving is anger. Grief can be caused by the death of a loved one, a divorce or breakup, or the loss of a career. The person who died, anybody else engaged in the event, or inanimate things may be the target of the rage. Other grieving sensations include shock, numbness, guilt, sadness, loneliness, and dread.

Post-traumatic stress disorder

People who were formerly sociable and friendly returned from battle angry and frequently violent. Domestic violence among former vets has grown massively. Some servicemen murdered their lovers or family members. Many individuals were taken aback, although research has long connected PTSD to emotions of rage and even violent aggressiveness. People suffering from PTSD may be furious over the trauma they experienced, or they may feel powerless or out of control. Posttraumatic stress disorder is commonly misunderstood as an anxiety problem. Many people imagine persons who are unable to leave their houses and are quickly triggered into panic or fear episodes. Anger, on the other hand, is a typical symptom of PTSD so prevalent, in fact, that it is expressly included as a common emotional reaction among persons with PTSD in the Diagnostic and Statistical Manual of

Mental Disorders (DSM-5). Anger might make it harder to receive help from loved ones. A person who is furious or out of control may feel guilty or humiliated, exacerbating the isolation caused by trauma. Trauma may be very isolating. Loved ones may be oblivious to the tragedy or respond improperly. Rape survivors, for example, commonly describe being quizzed about their own behavior, but returning troops claim that citizens are typically eager to inquire about violent war experiences. Even though loved ones strive to be supportive, they may not completely get the gravity of the trauma, leaving trauma survivors feeling neglected or forgotten. This might result in rage, distrust, and other negative feelings.

Problems in this section result in frequent outbursts of intense emotions, such as fury and anger. People suffering from PTSD may get stuck in their response to overwhelming threats. As a result, you may respond to every stress in survival mode. If you have PTSD, you may react to any stimuli with full activation. You may respond as if your life or self-esteem were in jeopardy. Anger and post-traumatic stress disorder (PTSD) frequently overlap. Anger is a common hyperarousal sign of PTSD, and it can have an impact on your interactions with others. It's critical to understand that the rage of persons suffering from PTSD can grow so severe that it feels out of control. When this occurs, you may become hostile towards others or even damage yourself. That doesn't always happen, and not everyone suffering from PTSD reacts violently. Remember that fury is simply one symptom of PTSD; in fact, it is not required for a PTSD diagnosis. Although it may be, it isn't necessarily violent. Often, someone with PTSD who experiences severe rage attempts to suppress it or hide it from others. This has the potential to escalate to self-destructive conduct. Anger and irritation are PTSD hyperarousal symptoms. Consider hyperarousal to be a condition of perpetual "fight or flight." This increased anxiety can cause multiple symptoms such as difficulty sleeping, irritability, and hypervigilance. Conflicts between countries have taught humans more about the effects of war on men and women serving in the military. Veterans are clearly at risk for a variety of mental health issues, including PTSD and intense rage. Anger might be difficult to understand at times. A returning soldier may be upset with politicians who do not comprehend combat, yet they may also be proud of their service. PTSD does not only refer to returning soldiers. For example, a birthing person who has been harmed by a doctor may be upset about both the abuse and the loss of a more positive birth experience. A child abuse victim may have strong sentiments of rage toward their abuser. An adult child abuse victim may love their parents yet be enraged by the trauma they endured as a kid. Anger and hatred can be tough to handle when you are experiencing mixed emotions. In other circumstances, a person may believe that their anger is undesirable or that they are unable to describe why or to whom they are furious. It might be tough to spend time with someone who is angry. Friends and family members of persons suffering from PTSD-related fury may get tired of coping with mood swings or furious outbursts. They may get compassion fatigue or perhaps decide to abandon their relationship with their loved ones. This can increase isolation and anger. Those who are angry with PTSD may feel humiliated and deserve their feelings. This complex mixture makes it difficult for them to express their feelings or experiment with new coping mechanisms. When a person is righteously angry about being mistreated, they may be unwilling to attempt meditation or other coping strategies. After all, they shouldn't have had to go through trauma and shouldn't have to deal with the consequences, the argument goes. While these emotions are understandable, they may also be highly self-defeating.

Working with your fear, sadness, or both can help you develop more skilled methods of dealing with your anger. For example, you could discover that you have unresolved grief. You may also discover that you are afraid of a particular consequence. That's useful information for you to deal with because it includes addressing a deeper need than anger. Working with the underlying fundamental emotions, in summary, is a method of reducing recurrent anger, creating more inner calm, and *promoting rational action.*

Do you find yourself consistent with any of the above medical conditions?

Yes   *No*

If you ticked yes above, have you sought medical help for this?

Yes   *No*

Make sure you speak to your trusted medical practitioner if any of the above medical conditions are drastically impacting your anger management.

Chapter 11:
Other Underlying Factors Affecting Anger

A part from underlying medical conditions and obvious circumstances, anger can be caused by a multitude of other factors, some of which you may not be aware of or have no control over. The following list outlines some of these factors and how they cause anger:

Childhood Trauma

High levels of rage, according to one school of thought, are tied to an inherent survival impulse. When confronted with a severe threat, humans frequently react with rage. Anger may help a person survive by redirecting his or her attention. The individual devotes all his or her attention, thought, and action to survival. Anger is a frequent reaction to situations that appear unfair or in which you have been made a victim. According to research, rage is especially likely when you have been betrayed by others. This is more common in circumstances of trauma involving exploitation or violence. The stress and shock of early childhood abuse frequently impact the survivor's ability to learn to manage his or her emotions.

Alcohol abuse

According to studies, drinking alcohol increases aggression. In some countries, alcohol is responsible for about half of all violent crimes. Alcohol abuse, commonly known as alcoholism, is defined as an overdose of alcohol at one time or on a regular basis. Alcohol inhibits your capacity to think clearly and rationally. It influences your impulse control and might make it difficult to regulate your emotions.

Drug Addiction

In rehabilitation, you learn to recognize your feelings, accept them for what they are, and then cope with them. Anger is one of the toughest feelings to deal with since it is frequently a mask for deeper, underlying feelings. However, if you understand how anger acts as a secondary emotion, you will be able to better identify what you are feeling and manage it. Anger may easily blind people and cause individuals to respond in less-than-optimal ways. During active addiction, people most certainly encounter instances in which they wish they had acted differently. Emotional regulation is an excellent technique to deal with this powerful feeling. Emotional control is a skill that takes time to master, yet it is useful when coping with complicated emotions like anger. Begin by understanding your emotions and how they affect you physically, cognitively, and emotionally. Then, consider what is driving you to feel this way. Once you've done that, you'll be able to accept your feelings and employ coping skills like grounding strategies to get through them. After that, you may consider how to prevent those emotions in the future or how to remedy the issue.

Genetics

Temperament is stable, especially in adulthood. Similar dispositions within the family can be traced back to shared genetics and the environment in which a person grows. When compared to their other siblings, identical twins often have similar temperaments. Even identical twins who were reared in separate families exhibit comparable characteristics. According to scientists, genetics accounts for 20-60% of the predisposition. Temperament does not have a defined inheritance pattern, and there are no unique genes that give certain temperamental features. Several genes that influence temperament have been found through large-scale investigations. Many of these genomes are involved in the communication of brain cells. Certain gene variants may lead to specific temperamental features.

Environmental Factors

Environmental variables influence gene activity, which influences temperament. Genes that enhance the likelihood of impulsive, temperamental features may be activated in children reared in an unpleasant environment, such as one of child abuse and violence. A kid who grows up in a pleasant environment, such as a safe and loving household, may have a calmer temperament, in part due to the activation of a distinct set of genes. Adolescent rage seems to be directly related to a home environment, especially family instability. Divorce and family disturbance appears to have long-term consequences on children's emotional health and increase their proclivity to battle anger issues as adults. Furthermore, persons who encounter intense violence, such as a war, are more prone to develop anger difficulties long after they come home.

Do you recall any environmental factors that are affecting your anger management, whether current or from the past? Describe these below.

_____

_____

_____

_____

_____

_____

Age

Advanced age carries with it new obstacles, such as loss of independence or the death of peers, that may not always have favorable responses. People are not served by reacting to such circumstances with rage. Anger is preferred over sorrow, fear, or despair because it feels more empowering. Anger shields them from the vulnerability of those underlying feelings. To make matters worse, anger is linked to greater levels of inflammation and chronic disease in persons aged 80 and up. While inflammation may be beneficial in fighting infection or damage, too much of it has been linked to health issues such as heart disease and dementia.

So the next time you feel angry, moderate, or strong, take a moment to look inside yourself to see if you can identify the underlying emotions that are causing your anger. If it's difficult to notice anything other than the fury, begin by investigating your ideas, as they are what feed all emotions. Keep in mind that the transition from a primary feeling such as fear or sadness to anger mode is usually quick and unconscious. You may have an entrenched pattern of feeling angry, which means it may take more effort to understand the underlying ideas and feelings that lay behind it. You can more readily select the appropriate course of action to tackle your situation if you identify the predominant emotion. For example, you can determine if another person's actions are unfair or merely a slap in the face to your ego. It is sensible to stand up to injustice, just as it is to prevent yourself or another from being taken advantage of or damaged. However, deciding to dispute with someone about something minor is motivated by ego. Putting emphasis on the latter is a waste of energy that may be better spent elsewhere.

Chapter 12:
Zodiac Signs and Anger

W hile everyone feels furious at some time in their life, some people struggle with anger. They lash out at others for no cause and are constantly enraged. It's difficult to have a conversation with them, and it's much more difficult to have constructive conversations with them because they'll turn it into an ugly argument. Our zodiac sign is an excellent approach to examining your personality qualities, particularly when it comes to expressing anger. A horoscope can only reveal so much information since no one is immune to the sentiments that come with rage, no matter how it manifests itself. When this kind of rage arises from deep inside you, it can be difficult to deal with sensitively.

If you feel like your zodiac sign says so much about you, here is an insight according to astrology and the zodiac signs that struggle to manage their anger most:

Aquarians are normally quite calm, and it takes a lot for them to become agitated. When Aquarius is upset, don't expect them to talk to you for a while since their first line of defense is to keep silent. You'll try to ignore the cause of your agitation for an extended period, perhaps, if possible, in the hope that you'll finally be able to calm down. If you can't, you'll spiral into a rage and eventually lose your cool. Even if you've released all your bad emotions, it may take some time for you to start talking to friends again.

A **Virgo** is also prone to irritability. If things don't go their way, they're prone to snapping at others. They believe in the power and are frequently disturbed when it does not occur. Virgos' anger has no bounds, and they frequently lose sight of who is in front of them when they are enraged. Virgos aren't very comfortable expressing their anger, so they keep it bottled up until you blow out, no matter how trivial the offense. Virgo's concealed rage frequently causes digestive and health problems. They feel incredibly misunderstood, and when your rage finally manifests itself, it may be perplexing and embarrassing for everyone. Their rage is generally directed at something that happened in the distant past rather than something that is happening today. If they can stop sobbing and banging doors, they can see that no one is out to get them.

An **Aries** is also known for having a lot of anger issues. They become enraged about little things, and their rage does not dissipate quickly. They prefer to harbor grudges, and their rage grows stronger with time. They don't forget quickly and are continually seeking retribution out of rage. Aries people are renowned for exploding without thinking about how their actions may influence others. They are not one to sugar-coat their emotions, and if they are upset with someone, they'd best be careful. Aries, one of the fire signs, is the most irritable of the zodiac signs. It doesn't help that their zodiac sign is the Ram, an angry animal. The fury is readily ignited, but it will swiftly die if the person they are yelling at doesn't react and remains calm. Aries can be easily enraged at times, yet, following an outburst, they typically calm down fast and feel extremely remorseful for their actions, but it won't stop them from exploding again later.

Libras are gentle; nevertheless, when they witness anything wrong, they become enraged. They have zero tolerance for injustice, and their moral principles come first. They have a great sense of self-worth and would go to any length to save it. If you are one, you avoid expressing your rage because you believe it is an unappealing emotion. It also frequently clashes with your pleasant and appealing character. While you strive to remain calm in the face of rage, you can't always talk yourself out of it and will eventually lose your cool. When you do lose it, though, you sincerely think that whatsoever you conveyed your anger was the greatest way conceivable. Libras have a tendency to explain everything, even while they're having a nervous breakdown.

When you're furious with someone, as a **Taurus,** you give them subtle indications initially, becoming quiet and distant before exploding with fiery wrath like a volcano. Taurus zodiac sign people don't get upset easily, but when they do, they frequently vent their rage by tossing things. You're also completely capable of losing your mind at any time. When you're enraged, no one should be in your line of fire.

Geminis love to talk, so it stands to reason that your preferred method of expressing anger is to fly off the handle by yelling, shouting, and throwing sarcastic and occasionally nasty comments. But, because you're known for having two personalities, yelling isn't the only method you use to show your rage. You may also remain calm and level-headed while blasting someone in the neck with the appropriate cutting insult. Whatever anybody does, they must not pass judgment on you or provide an opinion on what you should do with your life, or they will become the target of your anger.

When **Cancer** is upset, they sulk first; then, if no one notices, they move on to passive-aggressiveness before entirely retiring into their shell. When you're in protective shell mode, others should conclude that ignoring you is the best course of action because this is when you need love and kindness the most. If you're still not receiving what you need, your quiet rage will turn to tears, and if you're still not happy that no one is listening to your concerns, you'll make it rain. Every bottled-up emotion and unresolved rage from the past will be released.

When you're enraged, **Leo,** you move beyond fury and into a furious storm. You're not scared to yell, and the louder and more powerful your yelling, the better you feel. Because you are hot-tempered, Leo can be short-tempered at times. If someone says or does anything that irritates you, your go-to is swear words. When you're furious, you have a propensity to think primarily about your emotions, and people may assume you have anger issues as a result. While you may forgive someone for doing something that has enraged you, you are unlikely to apologize for your own actions.

Scorpios aren't readily angered, but when they are, people should do all they can to stay out of your way because you are terrifying when furious. Your stink-eye will send shivers down anyone's spine, and your snide remarks when enraged are cruel. You are not a sign who forgives and forgets, and you can never simply let things go when you are angry. People should be wary of the enraged Scorpio since the emotional havoc you unleash isn't beautiful.

Sagittarius is dominated by fire; therefore, it stands to reason that you will burn out rapidly if you are one. When you're furious, you use your words, but it doesn't make it any less terrible for those around you. If someone irritates you, it's natural for you to unfriend them right away, both on social media and in person, and then deal with your anger next. When you're upset, the easiest method for people to deal with you is to try to derail you since you have a propensity to digress so much that you forget why you're so enraged in the first place.

Capricorns, take anger extremely seriously, and you normally don't show it unless you're pushed to your breaking point. When given the opportunity, you are known to shatter whatever is handy and cut someone with criticism. They shouldn't be fooled by your calm manner since you'll claim people have disappointed you rather than express how furious you are with them. When you're pushed to an outburst, it's so out of character that everyone around you will be taken aback.

Pisces are continually affected by their emotions, which is a positive thing since it means you don't get angry very frequently. When you get upset, though, you can be downright scary, even if the only person you like to strike out at is yourself. When you're in a frenzy, you might become aggressive and self-destructive, and your creative imaginations go wild with the drama. Once your rage has subsided, you'll need some serious alone time to let your heart heal.

The above insightful information about zodiac signs and the way each of them reacts in their angry state can help you identify yourself with your anger, although this is not set in stone. Many believe that the zodiac sign describes them perfectly, while others pay little to no attention to astrology.

What Zodiac sign are you?

_____

_____

_____

_____

_____

_____

How do you relate to the above description of your Zodiac Sign?

Very Accurate

Slightly Accurate

Not quite there

Completely inaccurate

Chapter 13:
Identifying Triggers

D o you find it hard to keep your anger under control in certain situations? Have you ever encountered a situation when your rage appeared to spiral out of control in an instant? Maybe others think you're too sensitive, or you think they know how to get under your skin. If these resonate with you, it's likely that you're dealing with emotional triggers.

Knowing your anger triggers or the events and situations that make you angry is crucial because you'll be able to deal with your anger more successfully if you're prepared. Anticipating anger improves your capacity to express it in a more productive way. Anger triggers are like any other type of emotional trigger. It's a sensitive area of your emotions that might be triggered by a certain scenario, person, or issue. For everybody, various situations might elicit different feelings. The variation is in your life experience. Your brain is trained to behave in various ways because of the things you encounter in life. The list of things that can make you feel something is practically unlimited. It might be a specific word, an action, a location, or a person; the list is endless. It's whatever your brain identifies with a particular memory from your life. Triggers are problematic since you might not be aware of them. Your emotions are stimulated without your knowledge in these instances. To modify an anger trigger, you must first determine what is causing you to become enraged. The basis is awareness. You can start to heal if you're aware of what's causing your rage. Anger triggers are frequently the outcome of mental distress. The amount of work you'll have to accomplish will be determined by the trigger. Anger triggers frequently need going through bad or painful situations in your life. Things like being abused as a child, being attacked by someone, or being in a setting where your physical safety was in jeopardy are all common traumatic events linked to anger.

Here are some triggers you may want to keep an eye out for:

Unjust treatment

When something unjust happens to them, many individuals become angry, agitated, or even outraged. Unfair acts happen to everyone, and they happen rather frequently. From being cut on the road or while waiting in line at the cinema. Unfair grades at schools or salary increments at school are also examples of unjust treatments that can trigger off your anger. It doesn't matter how you respond to injustice; what counts is whether your reaction is moderate, productive, or out of proportion to the situation.

Adapting to time constraints and difficulties

The modern world is a fast-paced environment. People are under continual pressure to multitask and boost their job production. However, obstacles inevitably arise that inhibit growth. Leaving a little late for work and getting stuck in a large traffic jam are examples of such disruptions. You are running late for a flight and being subjected to an additional security check. Have family or friends text you regularly while you're at work. After being kept on hold for forty-five minutes, your call is abruptly disconnected. Isn't it frustrating when things like this happen? Yes, absolutely. They happen to everyone, though, and they happen regardless of what you do to prevent them. For some sorts of delays, you may be able to set restrictions in a beneficial way. You might be able to inform family members that you need them to stop texting you at work, for example. Nonetheless, several delays and disappointments are unavoidable. Allowing your anger to spiral out of control will not help; instead, it will overwhelm you with anxiety.

Dishonesty or disappointment

It's natural to feel frustrated, disturbed, or furious when someone lets you down, whether they break a commitment or just lie. And most people are exposed to these experiences on a regular basis throughout their lives. Consider the following scenarios and see if these trigger your anger: Your boyfriend or spouse betrays you, or your supervisor fails to promote or increase you as promised. A close friend forgets your birthday or fails to assist with the move as she promised. It's natural to get frustrated or even furious in response to all these triggers. However, you should strive to determine which situations occur most frequently

68

in your life and, more importantly, which ones give you the greatest rage.

When confronted with threats to one's self-esteem

People want to feel good about themselves in some way. Even those with low self-esteem dislike being ridiculed and judged. Some people experience unhappiness and self-loathing when their self-esteem is threatened, while others experience fury. These threats might be credible and justified, or they can be completely unjust. Receiving a poor grade or evaluation, being insulted or mistreated, making a mistake in front of others, spilling wine on your friend's carpet, being rejected, or not being selected for the sports team are all instances of self-esteem threats that can trigger anger.

Having to deal with prejudice and discrimination

Most people who are subjected to discrimination and prejudice feel helpless and unable to improve their circumstances. Irritation, fury, hatred, and even despair are some of their reactions. Discrimination or prejudice can take many forms, from subtle to deliberate. The following are the most prominent themes of discrimination: physical appearance, racism, sexism, religious convictions, and sexual orientation. You're surely aware that the list of prevalent biases might go on and on. Being intolerant or biased, or being the victim of intolerance or prejudice, can both cause anger.

Being assaulted

The world is filled with violence. Anger is a natural reaction to being the victim of violence or abuse, but some people also experience anxiety and sadness. In certain circumstances, chronic abuse turns victims into perpetrators. Abuse can take various forms, ranging from subtle to explicit. Abuse or assault can be classified into the following general categories: Domestic violence, whether physical or verbal, child abuse, assault, rape, or verbal intimidation are all examples. You might be the offender or the sufferer, as with prejudice and discrimination, and either situation can lead to a lot of rages. Evaluate yourself to see if you've been a perpetrator, a victim, or both and how this triggers your anger.

Snap over minor things

What is known as "observational learning" is one of the most potent ways humans learn during childhood and continues into maturity. Learning through role models is another way of putting it. Parents normally act as role models in their children's lives; however, it's possible that their form of role modeling was fighting and arguing about petty matters. You saw them and understood that the only way to communicate wants is via confrontation and conflict. During their childhoods, one or both of your parents most likely learned the same thing and in the same way. Unless the cycle is terminated, it is handed on from generation to generation. You want to break the cycle so that your children may learn a healthier way to cope, and you start expressing your anger in a healthier way. You may feel helpless when it comes to what you want and expect from others. All this ends in frustration since it is human nature to resist being screamed at. People continue to disappoint you instead of giving you what you want and need, adding fuel to the fire. Not entirely aware of what they are doing, yet many of their activities exist just outside of their full consciousness. Feeling helpless is a symptom of the "helpless and hopeless" mindset. That phenomenon is either a symptom or a cause of depression. So, in addition to external circumstances that cause your rage to erupt, there's a chance you're sad. Depression and rage are frequently accompanied by one another.

Now that the most common triggers have been outlined, it is time to start noticing the patterns in your anger outbursts based on the above practical examples. Being able to anticipate what scenarios may irritate you will be a huge help in keeping your anger in check. You can opt to avoid triggering circumstances altogether, or if that isn't feasible, you can prepare yourself with strategies to reduce the risk of losing control before entering potentially risky instances. It's also possible to have completely distinct triggers based on what you've learned from individuals and the environment around you. These aspects are determined by your personal experience and if you learned appropriate strategies to vent your emotions. Anger may stew inside a person until it bursts if those traits are not actioned.

With how many triggers do you find yourself relating?

_____

_____

_____

_____

_____

List them below

_____

_____

_____

_____

_____

_____

_____

_____

The Anger diary

An anger diary or notebook may be a helpful tool for keeping track of your angry experiences. Make regular notes in your journal to record the incidents that have triggered you. There are specific sorts of information you'll want to note for each triggering occurrence to make the journal most useful:

- *What occurred that made you so enraged?*
- *What was the situation's provocative aspect?*
- *What were the feelings that ran through your head?*
- *On a scale of 0 to 100, how would you rate your anger? How enraged were you?*
- *What effects did your actions leave on you and others?*
- *Were you already apprehensive, tense, and under pressure from another situation? If that's the case, what was it that made you like this?*
- *What was your body's reaction? Did you notice your palms sweaty and your heart racing? Make a list of the physical changes.*
- *Did you want to run away from the stress or smash something?*
- *Did you have the urge to yell, or did you catch yourself slamming doors or being sarcastic?*
- *What exactly did you do?*
- *How did you feel just after the episode ended?*
- *Did you feel differently the next day or later?*
- *What were the outcomes of this incident?*

Review your journal after a week or so of writing this material and search for recurring themes or triggers that irritate you. Triggers can be classified into various categories, including:

- Other individuals are either doing or not doing what you anticipate.
- Traffic delays, computer troubles, ringing phones, and other situations that obstruct your progress.
- Those that take advantage of you

- Being enraged and dissatisfied with yourself
- Any of the aforementioned, in combination

Keep an eye out for anger-inducing thoughts that come up repeatedly. You will know these ideas since they usually revolve around one or more of the following topics:

- The belief that you have been cheated or mistreated.
- The notion that the person who provoked you intended to hurt you on purpose.
- The conviction that the other person did something wrong, that they should have acted differently, that they were evil or foolish for causing you suffering.

Use your anger journal to keep track of times when you were offended, why you thought the act was done on purpose, and why you thought it was wrong. Tracking your thinking patterns can assist you in identifying recurring themes in your life. The idea that people are acting this way and that you have every right to be angry with them is at the root of all trigger thoughts. Most people have a few ideas that regularly make them angry. Look for scenarios that make you angry and try if you can pinpoint the specific collection of triggering thoughts that makes you angry. Your diary's objective is to assist you in identifying patterns of behavior and particular repeating components that irritate you. The more closely you can watch your thoughts and behaviors, and the more complete your anger journal is, the higher chance you have of recognizing anger triggers and how you react to them. Understanding how you react to rage might help you devise tactics for dealing with your emotions in a more constructive manner. You'll be able to work more constructively to manage your response to triggers once you've recognized some of your triggers and begin to grasp your trigger patterns. Anger-inducing ideas come effortlessly and very instantly, so recognizing them and replacing them with something more beneficial will take some deliberate effort on your side. When you feel compelled in your anger, you are giving yourself permission to be furious, regardless of whether it's appropriate. The sooner you stop rationalizing your rage, the faster it will fade away. While all anger is valid in the sense that it reflects how you feel at the time, this does not always imply that acting on your angry sentiments is always acceptable. Remember that getting angry is unhealthy for your health and damaging to your crucial connections with others if you don't manage it properly.

The Anger worksheet

If you feel like an anger diary won't work for you and you prefer to log single incidents in separate worksheets, here is a sample of a worksheet you could use for this:

The anger worksheet

1	2	3	4	5	6	7	8	9	10

Anger scale

Describe the incident briefly:

_____

_____

_____

_____

_____

_____

What thoughts ran through your head?

_____

_____

_____

_____

_____

_____

_____

What were your actions?

_____

_____

_____

_____

_____

What do you think has triggered this rage? (for example, someone ridiculed you, you discovered someone lied to you, someone mistreated you)

_____

_____

_____

_____

_____

Could there have been an already-present trigger that worsened your reaction to this experience? If yes, what was it?

_____

_____

_____

_____

_____

List any physical characteristics you noticed during this rage.

_____

_____

_____

What urges did you experience? (The desire to yell, smash things, leave, etc.)

_____

_____

_____

What did you actually do?

_____

_____

_____

_____

How did you feel after it ended?

_____

_____

_____

_____

What is the outcome of this incident?

_____

_____

_____

_____

_____

How do you think you could have reacted any differently?

_____

_____

_____

_____

_____

Could this incident have been avoided altogether?

_____

_____

_____

_____

_____

Chapter 14:
19 Simple Ways You Can Do to Control Your Anger as a Woman

I s your blood pressure rising when your teenager refuses to comply? Anger that has spun out of control can be harmful to your health and relationships. When you're upset, it's tough to retain your calm. Use these basic techniques to deal with your rage:

1. It's easy to say something you later feel sorry for, and you only say it in the heat of the moment. Before you let your rage take control of the situation, take a few seconds to gather your thoughts and let everyone engaged in the issue do the same. When you're furious, it's tempting to let go of your rage, but you're more likely to cause harm than good. Pretend you're a kid again, with your lips sealed shut. This period of silence will allow you to collect your thoughts. The initial thought that appears in your mind when you are upset is probably not the best to say. Give yourself time before responding. This time will assist you in being calmer and more collected.

2. As soon as you're thinking clearly, express your disagreement in an assertive yet level-headed manner. Express your concerns and desires clearly and honestly without offending others or seeking to influence them.

3. Physical exercise can help with stress reduction, which contributes to rage. If you anticipate rage is growing, go for a brisk walk or run or spend some time doing other pleasurable physical activities. Exercise helps you relax and reduce frustration. Go for a walk, ride a bike or play golf. Everything that stimulates the limbs is good for the mind and body.

4. Work on fixing the situation at hand rather than dwelling on what got you angry. Remind yourself that anger will not solve your problems and may perhaps make them worse. It's preferable to focus your energy and emotions on something healthy and constructive rather than just being angry. Thus, it's

best to focus on actioning the issue rather than just getting angry.

5. Use phrases that put you in the center, like "I", in order to express yourself rather than criticizing or putting the blame on others. This will only add to the present stress. Respect and precision are key factors in communication here. If you express your feelings properly, it's okay. With the help of a good friend, you are responsible for finding a calm answer. Outbursts don't fix problems, but adult conversation can help you relax and calm down. It may also help to avoid future issues.

6. The ability to forgive is a powerful tool. Allowing anger and other negative emotions to override positive feelings may result in bitterness or a sense of injustice. If, alternatively, you can forgive someone who has mistreated you, you will be able to benefit from the experience while also deepening your bond. It takes a lot of emotional power to forgive those who hurt you. If you can't go that far, at least try to forgive them, and you'll see your anger disappear.

7. Relaxation might be facilitated by easing up the tension through humor. Use humor to cope with whatever is causing you to be upset, as well as any unrealistic assumptions you may have about how things should go. A positive attitude may turn a terrible day around. Find opportunities to laugh, whether it's playing with your kids, watching stand-up comedy, or browsing through memes. Sarcasm should be avoided since it might hurt feelings and make matters worse.

8. Put your relaxation techniques to use when your anger rises. Deep breathing exercises, visualizing a soothing landscape, or repeating a calming word or phrase can all help you relax. You may relax by listening to music, writing in a journal, or doing a few yoga poses, whatever it takes. As you become angrier, your breathing becomes shallower and faster. Take several calm, deep breaths from your nose and exhale through your mouth to reverse the flow and your anger. Non-strengthening yoga-like moves such as neck and shoulder rolls can help you regulate your body and manage your emotions. There's no need for specialized equipment.

9. Look for a word or phrase that might help you relax and refocus. When you're unhappy, repeat that term to yourself again and over. 'Relax" and "you'll be OK" are all good examples.

10. Put yourself in a peaceful room, close your eyes, and imagine yourself in a pleasant situation. Concentrate on the specifics in the hypothetical setting and utilize this time to escape the situation mentally and temporally. Allow yourself to relax. Take a seat away from the crowd. You can digest events and bring your emotions to neutral during this peaceful period. You may find time away from others so beneficial that you want to include it in your daily schedule.

11. You can write what you cannot express. Make a list of how you feel and how you want to react. It might help you calm down and examine the circumstances that led up to your anger if you write it down. This is when a journal or an anger worksheet comes in handy.

12. Prepare for an outburst by practicing what you'll say or how you'll address the matter in the future. This repeat interval also allows you to schedule a range of different responses.

13. When you're furious, the universal symbol for stop (stop sign) might help you relax. It's a quick approach to envision the necessity to stop yourself and your behaviors and leave the situation.

14. Find a different route if your stagnant commute to work gets you upset before you've even had your coffee. If meeting a group of friends makes you irritated or angry, politely voice your opinion and make sure you meet on time next time. Consider alternatives that result in less stress in the long run. You have a say in most of the things you do, and wherever possible, choose to change your routine if that's what's making you angry. People are prone to be enraged over the same things again and again. Think about what has made you furious for some time. If at all feasible, try to prevent or cope with certain situations. This point ties strongly to identifying your triggers wherever possible because there will always be unforeseeable circumstances that are going to make you angry, and these are out of your control.

15. When things don't seem right, take a minute to focus on what is right, like referring back to how many excellent things you have in your life might help you overcome your anger and turn things around.

16. Do your best to empathize and put yourself in the shoes of the other person and see the issue from their eyes. You may gain new insight and be less angry if you tell stories or experience events as they happened. Produce a physical item out of your rage. When you're sad, try painting, gardening, or composing. Feelings may be an incredible muse for inventive people. Utilize yours to calm down.

17. Anger might make you believe that things are much worse than they are. Replace negative ideas with more realistic ones to calm down. This can be accomplished by avoiding strong remarks or seize thinking about what might happen. Even if the matter has been handled, you may find yourself replaying the same scenario that angered you. Dwelling encourages anger to fester, potentially leading to further disputes or other problems. Attempt to move on from the source of your rage. Instead, focus on the good aspects of the person or scenario that has offended you.

18. Sleep is a crucial aspect of life, and getting enough of it can help you deal with a variety of physical, mental, and emotional issues, including anger. The body and mind relax and repair damaged cells and neural connections when we sleep. Everyone knows that getting a restful sleep makes individuals feel better. Although everyone is different and may require sleep than this, the ideal amount of excellent quality sleep is around seven hours every night.

These are simple ways you can go for whenever you feel like your anger is spiraling out of control. These are not long-term changes you can employ to change your reaction to a situation that usually makes you angry, but they are quick fixes for when you find yourself about to get involved in an angry situation. Progressive muscle relaxation entails tensing and gently relaxing different muscle groups in your body one by one. Take deep, deliberate breaths as you clench and relax.

Which ways will you be employing next to help control your anger?

_____

_____

_____

_____

_____

_____

_____

_____

_____

_____

_____

_____

_____

_____

Chapter 15:
Dealing With Anger in the Long-Term

S creaming and yelling aren't the only ways to express anger. Individuals that are angry might become threatening and aggressive. They have the potential to harm themselves, others, or property. Furthermore, some people feel horrible about their anger, which can lead to guilt. Anger that is out of control and excessive produces issues in many aspects of life. It can cause issues in relationships with friends, family, and co-workers. Anger that is out of control might lead to legal issues. However, not everyone who is upset shows it. Angry people may not express their rage externally. Anger may elicit a variety of responses. Anger could cause some instant responses. People, for example, are more prone to avoid angry people since being the target of rage is unpleasant. Angry people may get headaches, digestive problems, and other symptoms. In the long run, further effects of rage may arise. People who keep their anger bottled up may retreat, grumble, and ruminate. They may be in a state of mental distress and unrest. They have poorer self-esteem and greater anxiety and are more likely to abuse alcohol and drugs than persons who are less angry. Anger that isn't managed can lead to heart disease, high blood pressure, and cancer, as well as relationship and professional issues.

Apart from learning instant skills and ways how to manage anger there and then, one must make some lifestyle changes to minimize anger overall. If you are a woman who is often faced with pressure at work, at home, or in your relationship for the reasons mentioned earlier, you are more likely to find yourself losing it or suppressing your anger, more time than you can count. First and foremost, understand that rage is a typical and occasionally healthy human emotion. It is acceptable to get angry sometimes. When anger becomes excessive, uncontrollable, or related to dysfunctional behaviors, it becomes an issue that may influence every aspect of one's life. Second, keep in mind that furious behavior patterns are formed, repeated, and reinforced over time. These behaviors, fortunately, can be corrected. Anger is an innate emotional response that may be lessened with work. You cannot lash out at every person or anything that upsets or annoys you; laws, societal rules, and common sense all restrict how far our rage may go. People deal with their furious sentiments through a range of conscious and unconscious mechanisms. Expressing, repressing, and calming are the three major techniques. The healthiest method to express rage is to express it in a proactive rather than aggressive manner. To do so, you'll need to learn how to express your expectations clearly and how to have them satisfied without causing harm to others. Being assertive does not imply being forceful or demanding; rather, it entails treating yourself and others with respect. Anger can be suppressed, transformed, or redirected after it has been restrained. This occurs when you suppress your rage, stop thinking about it, and concentrate on something constructive. The goal is to control or repress your anger so that it may be diverted into more productive conduct. The risk with this sort of reaction is that if it isn't allowed to outwardly express itself, it will turn inward on itself.

Finally, by constructively managing your anger, you can relax on the inside. This entails not only managing your external actions but also your internal responses, such as lowering your heart rate, calming yourself down, and allowing your emotions to escape. The following are some approaches you can start adopting to control your anger in the long run:

Cognitive behavior therapy (CBT Approach)

Cognitive-behavioral therapy (CBT) is a solution-focused type of psychotherapy that teaches you how to recognize negative thoughts and feelings, conduct a reality check, then challenge and replace those thoughts with more sensible ones. Because it focuses on practical methods to help you feel better, it's beneficial for individuals with anxiety, depression, anger challenges, stress, and addiction. The ideas and feelings surrounding an action are examined through functional analysis. The focus of analysis is not just on the ideas that lead to certain behaviors but also on the triggers for those thoughts. New coping abilities that can be employed in everyday life are the objective of skills training as part of this approach. A CBT therapist will participate actively in your sessions, providing you with direct feedback and advice. They'll also give you tasks, such as maintaining a daily mood diary, to help you become more aware of the negative claims you make to yourself and understand how those ideas affect your moods and behavior. It's crucial to remember that altering negative thinking patterns and actions takes time; the key is to practice the approaches consistently. CBT uses a series of questions and activities to help you understand the triggers that cause anger to increase and result in outbursts. Your therapist can teach you skills to handle anger more successfully once you've identified the triggers and their core sources, such as deep breathing, relaxation techniques, and problem-solving. CBT for rage also emphasizes the need for forceful, calm discourse over aggressive, unhealthy communication. Remember that wrath is a normal human emotion that should be expressed when warranted. The goal is to create adaptive techniques for expressing rage that does not go beyond appropriate boundaries.

In essence, cognitive-behavioral therapy is a science-based therapeutic method that encourages rational thinking and provides clients with skills to improve their mental and emotional well-being. CBT is one of the most popular and useful treatments for anger management, according to most specialists. Clients learn to detect patterns that lead to exaggerated emotions by investigating the thought-emotion-behavior triangle. The following are some of the CBT techniques used by your therapist:

Reorganization of the mind

How you understand an incident that causes you to be angry or dissatisfied will determine how you react. You learn to understand situations differently through cognitive restructuring, which changes how you react to rage. The idea isn't to eliminate anger from your emotional spectrum or to establish a more optimistic perspective. There are occasions when the rage is a reasonable emotion, as described before. Anger, on the other hand, might become the driving force behind a proactive attitude if you find out a method to logically assess the situation and express emotions in a practical and socially acceptable manner. The way you view a circumstance that makes you angry will have a direct influence on how you respond to it. You learn to recognize harmful thinking patterns that feed your anger and replace them with more reasonable, balanced beliefs through cognitive restructuring. A thought log is an important tool in CBT since it allows you to keep a record of comments you make to yourself as well as what triggers them. A CBT therapist may give you homework to track and document negative thoughts and triggers that you aren't always aware of. You will develop a deeper insight into what you are thinking and how these thoughts affect how you behave as you continue to utilize the diary. You'll be able to question the ideas and replace them with good ones, or just observe them and let them go, rather than responding in anger. This is a fantastic method to approach challenges from a new viewpoint. The way you think might sometimes build roadblocks between you and the solution. As part of your natural survival instinct, your brain is hard-wired to seek out and focus on threats. This encourages negative thinking, in which you concentrate solely on the problem. A more positive outcome is probable if you consciously change your mental process to focus on objectives and the activities you may take to attain them rather than continually focus on the problem. When you have a problem, the counselor will assist you in recognizing your thoughts and behavioral patterns. The therapist will ask you to pay great attention to your emotions, behaviors, and bodily responses during the session. You'll need to consider if your views are skewed or realistic at this stage. Based on your emotions, you may see life experiences as either negative or positive. CBT aids in the re-framing of memories. This time is difficult for many people. Healthy thought and positive conduct, on the other hand, can be established through CBT.

Problem-solving skills

A CBT therapist will assist you in implementing strategic techniques to solve the situation. Rather than taking your angry reactions out on everyone around you, it's critical to have a problem-solving purpose. This looks to include being adaptable in your thinking and transforming angry ideas into more constructive ones. It also weighs the risks and rewards of continuing to view the situation with rage.

Communication skills

Excessive anger sufferers frequently hide their sentiments until they are vented in a turbulent, inappropriate manner. Both verbal and nonverbal conduct is targeted by assertive communication. The emphasis in verbal communication is on what has really been stated and the usage of "I" expressions. Eye contact, posture, tone of voice, the volume of speech, and contemplative listening are all examples of nonverbal communication. A CBT therapist can assist you in developing assertiveness skills. Communication is essential for effective problem solving, especially whether the issue is a relationship or a societal issue that involves others. Because the attention turns from fixing the problem to either criticizing the other person or protecting oneself from criticism, anger inhibits the free flow of thoughts. Neither position is favorable to effective communication. Consider what you're saying and how you're saying it. This is an excellent strategy to avoid getting into a fight with someone. You're less likely to grow upset and furious if you can convey your sentiments effectively, and the other person is less likely to react with anger as well.

Creating Awareness

An important component of dealing with anger issues is self-awareness. When someone is furious, it affects their ideas and viewpoint. After you've identified the issues you're dealing with, you'll need to discuss everything that's on your mind. The therapist will emphasize the significance of talking to oneself. Self-reflection has the benefit of allowing you to reflect on and uncover your physical and emotional responses to a challenging scenario. The key principle is to increase self-awareness and a better understanding of how misguided judgments can lead to rash actions and outbursts of anger. The problem with anger is that it confuses our judgment and makes it difficult to contain ourselves long enough to find a healthy method to express it.

In a nutshell, here is what to expect from CBT sessions for anger management:

- Your therapist can assist you in identifying the conditions that are causing you problems. This will support you in making a more informed decision about which problem and objective you should address first. In essence, you're trying to figure out what's causing your rage. Childhood trauma, marital problems, and the death of a loved one could all be examples of this.
- An important component of dealing with anger challenges is self-awareness. When someone is furious, it affects their ideas and perception. After you've identified the issues you're dealing with, you'll need to discuss everything that's on your mind. The therapist will emphasize the significance of talking to oneself. Introspection has the benefit of allowing you to reflect on and uncover your physical and emotional responses to a challenging scenario. This step should help increase your self-awareness and your understanding of the situation.
- When you have a problem, the therapist can assist you in recognizing your thoughts and behavioral patterns. The therapist will ask you to pay great attention to your emotions, behaviors, and bodily responses during the process. This will help you distinguish between the negative and unrealistic thoughts as opposed to the helpful ones.
- You'll need to consider if your views are twisted or genuine at this stage. Based on your emotions, you may see life experiences as either negative or favorable. CBT aids in the re-framing of memories. This step is difficult for many people. Healthy thought and positive conduct, on the other hand, can be established through CBT. Ultimately here, you should be able to change negative thoughts and work on them constructively. This therapy process is not there to alienate negative completely

89

from your head but to deal with them differently when they appear.

Solution-focused brief therapy (SFBT)

This can assist you in identifying exceptions to your anger issues and making appropriate modifications as a result. What was different about the occasions when you were able to properly handle triggers or sensations that would normally have you become furious? Once you've determined and comprehended what was different, you may start doing more of what has or did work during those exceptions on purpose. This is a collaborative goal-directed method of psychotherapy transformation that involves direct observation of clients' replies to a series of carefully designed questions. Solution-building rather than problem-solving is the focus of this strength-based approach to psychotherapy. SFBT is different from other types of psychotherapy in that it focuses on how your current circumstances and future hopes affect you. Together with your therapist, and depending on their qualifications, they will choose the best approach to help you.

Other anger management therapy approaches

Dialectical behavioral therapy (DBT) is a type of CBT that can assist people with acute or regular anger to regain emotional control by teaching them emotional regulation and distress tolerance skills, as well as mindfulness and effective interpersonal communication. Family therapy is a type of treatment that can be beneficial in circumstances when anger is frequently directed against family members. It can assist you in working together to enhance communication and problem-solving. Psychodynamic treatment can assist you in examining the psychological basis of your anger and your response to it to discover and address problematic behaviors. Your mental healthcare professional will assess your circumstances and individual habits to establish the overall treatment plan and whether medication is required in addition to counseling. Understanding your causes and responses to anger, learning skills to manage or defuse it, and altering beliefs and attitudes about anger; are all examples of anger management treatment practices. Anger management treatment can teach you techniques to regulate your anger by avoiding it or distracting yourself from it. Your therapist can assist you in determining how to respond when you are angry. Role-playing allows you to practice skills like assertiveness and direct communication, which may help you gain control. Therapy may also teach you coping methods and relaxation techniques like slow deep breathing, leaving the room and returning when you're calm, or utilizing a peaceful image to reduce the intensity of your anger.

Anger management therapy can assist you in identifying and changing negative thought patterns that fuel your anger. Knowing what situations elicit your rage might assist you in avoiding them or managing your reaction to them. Therapy can help you manage your emotions, control your behaviors, and build coping skills for circumstances that make you angry. Your therapist may coach you on relaxation techniques to help you slow down and relax your body and mind. If events continually elicit your rage, your therapist may push you to seek answers or alternatives. Anger management treatment can assist you in expressing your emotions in a healthy, polite, or forceful manner that is not confrontational.

Which therapy approaches do you feel most comfortable trying?

_____

_____

_____

_____

_____

_____

_____

This is If therapy is something you want to use to control your anger.

Lifestyle change

Your surroundings may not always be a nice and good place to be, which can have a bad impact on your mood and lead you to get anxious, upset, and furious. If your rage is caused by a hostile work environment, it may be time to change jobs. Most of the time, though, the situation isn't as difficult as it appears. It's possible that you're simply overworked, exhausted, and in need of a break. In such a situation, take some time off, go on a vacation, and remember to shift your mindset and concentrate on your other skills when you return. Other times you may experience anger because of things you either have direct control over or concerns created through things you have indirect control over. You have control over your commitments, your productivity at work, your reputation through your actions, whom you choose to follow on your social media platform, whom you meet for coffee, and whom you spend your time with. You should not dwell on the things you have no control over. For these things, you should focus on changing your response to them because you have already established that these things cannot be changed from your end. For the things you CAN change, then you should focus on changing your circle if the people around you are making you angry or frustrated. Politely refuse a coffee meet-up with a friend that does nothing but transpose negative energy onto you. If a commitment you have taken up is making you angry or stressed out, politely refuse it, or delegate the work when possible. If your partner is making your relationship abusive and making you angry, choose to go the other way. If you want things to change, put in the work and change them.

Music

Individuals with anger management difficulties or other illnesses have been shown to benefit from music therapy and its remedies. Music therapy can help people who have trouble controlling their anger or who have a condition that makes it difficult to regulate their emotions. Lyrical analysis, song writing, dance, and movement performance, as well as any other music therapy therapies often utilized to aid individuals with anger management difficulties, might yield favorable effects.

Although music isn't usually associated with anger management, it may be a useful tool in learning to handle powerful emotions like rage. Clearly, the overall goal of employing music therapy for anger management is to assist people in better managing their emotions. However, there are several minor goals that contribute to the achievement of the larger goal. These objectives range from recognizing the memories or experiences that cause anger to build a system of anger management skills. These objectives assist people in determining the source of their rage outbursts or moments of uncontrollable rage, as well as developing healthy reactions to their triggers. Music therapy is a diverse discipline with a range of intervention strategies depending on the client's needs. Some therapies are used to attain goals in anger management and the processing of negative emotions. A lyrical analysis is one of the therapeutic strategies utilized in prisons. Clients can engage with and evaluate the lyrics of well-known songs using lyrical analysis. Clients can then examine their own ideas and feelings in response to the lyrics' substance. This allows people to connect with their emotions.

The way music expresses emotions via the narrative you hear in songs can help people become more aware of your feelings and the various ways you can express them. The first step in any anger management strategy is to become aware of your emotions. For many people, listening to music for anger issues can provide a sense of well-being. Music can help a person relax or become more conscious of their emotions. Many people suffer from physical problems because of unhealthy anger, such as hypertension. Hypertension can be reduced by listening to music when they're angry. Music may be used to help with anger control in a variety of ways. One approach for helping patients regulate their anger is to listen to genres of music. Others find that composing music is the most effective kind of treatment for their anger issues. Anger management therapists and behavioral specialists frequently use music in their therapy strategies. This may inspire patients to recollect events that have had an influence on their lives and to target the positive aspects of their life. They may relate when listening to music. This can assist them in working through their disappointment and anger in a productive manner. Therefore, healthy rage can take the place of destructive or violent conduct. Various forms of music may be recommended by therapists and specialists to address certain anger issues. Songs depicting sentiments of sadness over a broken relationship, for example, could be beneficial to persons experiencing addictive anger. People who exhibit explosive anger may benefit from listening to music that depicts resistance and despair. Other sorts of music may encourage self-healing by encouraging positive thinking and reinforcement.

Different music genres have various effects on different people. Some people feel that listening to religious, traditional, or orchestral relaxes them. Others feel that listening to angst-ridden songs might help them relax. Anger management is often aided by performing music, whether publicly or privately. Composing music and song lyrics may help many musicians communicate sentiments of deep-seated anger or despair. As a result, those who utilize music as a productive outlet may be able to cope with anger better. If you find songs that relax you and calm your rage, create a playlist on your phone and keep it handy for when your next rage attack takes over. If you are currently undergoing therapy for anger management, feel free to suggest this approach to your therapist if they do not already use it.

How helpful do you find music to be when you are enraged?

_____

_____

What music genre do you choose during these moments?

_____

_____

_____

Journaling

Journaling is the activity of maintaining a written record that examines your thoughts and feelings about life's experiences. This form of a journal is useful for anybody dealing with transitory anger difficulties because of stressful life events such as moving, changing employment, or the death of a loved one. Anger management journals, on the other hand, are particularly beneficial in assisting people with and stopping the cycle of chronic anger. Individuals who experience continuous, frequent, and uncontrolled bouts of rage that may endanger their physical, emotional, and mental health are also included. There are various approaches to this. Journaling, as an anger control and self-exploration technique, should be done on a regular basis or whenever you feel the need to journal. Writing in detail about feelings and thoughts connected to stressful situations, as one would discuss themes in therapy and develop solutions, is one of the most effective strategies to reduce anger using journaling. It enables you to clarify your ideas and feelings, acquiring vital self-awareness. It's also a useful problem-solving tool; on paper, one can frequently hash through an issue and come up with answers more quickly. An anger journal is a valuable tool for tracking your angry episodes. Make daily entries or entries as soon as you feel irritated. In your journal, write down the instances that irritated you. To make the journal most valuable, you'll want to record specific sorts of information for each inciting incident, like what enraged you, scaling your anger, what was going through your mind when this happened and how this affected your behavior. Recording this information for a few weeks or so will allow you to identify recurring themes or triggers that prompted you to become enraged. The goal of journaling is to assist you in identifying patterns of behavior and certain repeating items that "push your buttons." The more precisely you can recognize your thoughts and behaviors, the more probable it is that you identify anger triggers. Because of this, you should be able to respond to them favorably. Understanding how you feel angry might help you devise tactics for dealing with your emotions in more constructive ways. Journaling may improve your behavior and well-being if it forces you to take a step back and assess your thoughts, feelings, and behavior while also assisting you in exploring answers. It will assist you in aligning your emotions and motives with your deepest objectives while also converting negative energy into good creativity and progress. Journaling reduces your emotional reaction toward people. It Increases tolerance for ambiguity, uncertainty, and instability, all of which are typical aspects of life. It also allows you to perceive other people's points of view alongside your own, making you feel more empathetic. Making a record of your furious outbursts will assist you in deciding on a plan of action. Writing in an anger management notebook helps the brain concentrate its ideas by allowing for deliberate and purposeful expression. Even simply writing what triggered your rage or how it made you feel might help you regain intellectual and emotional control. At the same time, writing about feelings of anger and who or what caused it is not enough to create a sense of dissolution and long-term control. Anger management journals need to have the structure and focus on making this kind of progress, rather than simply filling in blank pages with insults, losses, and frustration details.

There is no perfect approach to making an anger management journal. However, there are three critical components for peak effectiveness and ultimate peace of mind:

Acknowledgment

There is no way to find a healthy remedy before a person recognizes that there is a problem. This isn't to say that your writing in the anger management diary should read like a confession of anything you've done wrong. Instead, identify the facts around your anger, including who or what was involved, when or where it occurred, how or why your anger was aroused, and a description of your anger in terms of an emotional reaction. It can be hard to recall the details of the situation and your emotional reactions, especially if you keep an anger management journal at the end of the day. However, the more information and details you provide, the clearer your picture of what happened and how you behave will be. You are validating yourself with this admission, and with this viewpoint, you are allowing yourself to perceive the issue and your anger with more clarity.

Self-Compassion

People who do not battle with chronic anger may be surprised at how hard those who do are on themselves. Many people who are naturally furious turn those angry sentiments on themselves, resulting in a grueling and exhausting cycle of rage and regret. That is why reflecting self-compassion in your anger management notebook is essential. After you've acknowledged your anger, it's critical to show compassion for yourself. This is not to say that you should wipe the slate clean or disregard any bad effects of your rage. Acknowledgment, together with the resultant viewpoint, leads to learning and improvement. Self-compassion, on the other hand, is a journaling approach that helps you to break the cycle of anger and regret. You can include in your journal post that all humans get angry and make errors and that you are working on regulating your feelings and gaining control of your anger. This is a process, and writing such reminders to yourself can help you to be more open to accepting and offering compassion and forgiveness. What is frequently misunderstood about compassion and forgiveness is that it relieves the giver as well as the receiver. That's why there are so many memorable proverbs about letting go of grudges and wrath. When you exercise self-compassion and self-forgiveness, you strengthen your ability to provide compassion and forgiveness to others, easing your emotional weight.

Mindful action

Similar to how identifying an issue is the first step toward regulating and controlling your anger, journaling about mindful or thoughtful action can provide a feeling of resolution and help you to go ahead. This does not imply that you must devise a method to fix or repair the consequence of your anger, though this may be an option on occasion. Creating an entry that represents mindful behavior, on the other hand, should contain a coping method other than rage. You can, for example, look at your acknowledgment and self-compassion and write down the reaction you wish you had instead, or a suggestion for how to remind your future self to halt and breathe before allowing anger to dominate you. If you find that you have made progress in regulating your anger, take advantage of the chance to acknowledge to yourself a noticeable improvement in selecting attentive and intelligent activities over furious emotions. Even thinking about the fact that you took the time to write an entry in your anger management diary is a mindful action. If those feelings reappear, or if you become stuck recalling and reliving specific events that prompted you to feel angry, you may return to this section of your entry and remind yourself to go ahead in your activities rather than loop back and disrupt your progress.

Anger management journals can help you regulate your anger by offering an intellectual and analytical perspective rather than an emotional one. It is an opportunity for you to take charge of how you respond to yourself in the future by admitting the problem, practicing self-compassion, and choosing more attentive and purposeful action. This logical, non-judgmental, forgiving, and progressive approach will help you understand who you are, whom you have the potential to be, and how far you have progressed on your path. Not only will the journaling process be satisfying, but you will also be rewarded by feeling better physically, psychologically, and emotionally as your sense of control over your anger grows. Keeping an anger management notebook is a commitment to your health and well-being. It may be difficult to detect the physical toll that your anger is having on your body's systems until something dramatic occurs. Furthermore, being consumed by anger has a negative impact on your personal and professional connections, which can significantly affect your emotional well-being through rejection and isolation. Perhaps more crucially, frequent, prolonged, and severe anger alters and poisons a person's worldview. This decreases trust, compassion, and openness toward others. People in a natural state of rage, on the other hand, have a heightened awareness that the world is an adversarial, unforgiving, and untrustworthy place. An anger management journal will not stop you from feeling furious in the future, nor will it offer you complete control over this normal and natural human emotion. However, if you utilize this form of notebook properly and consistently, you will be able to manage your anger in better ways and regulate it so that it isn't an oppressive and damaging aspect of your life. It's crucial to emphasize that if you believe your anger is endangering your own or someone else's health and well-being, you should seek professional treatment right away.

Anger management Journal
This can be used to record single incidents of rage.

Date:

(Make sure you fill out this entry as soon as the incident happens)

Scale your anger

1-not too angry

2- a little angry

3- angry

4-very angry

5-highly angry

Trigger:

(Describe in detail what has triggered your anger)

_____

_____

_____

_____

Anger management technique used in this incident

_____

_____

_____

_____

Scale your anger after using this technique/approach

1-not too angry

2- a little angry

3- angry

4-very angry

5-highly angry

Weekly Anger management journal

An anger journal is a tool for reflecting on and learning from hostile experiences. Journaling is also beneficial to one's mental health. It is beneficial to discuss everyday stressors in a secure setting and to process them without tension. This will enable you to improve your problem-solving skills. Use this format if you feel like you encounter triggers on a daily basis.

Remember what the triggers were. What would you do in a different manner if you could go back in time?

Week starting:

Monday

_____

_____

_____

Tuesday

_____

_____

_____

Wednesday

_____

_____

_____

Thursday

_____

_____

_____

Friday

_____

_____

_____

Saturday

_____

_____

_____

_____

_____

_____

Breathing Techniques

When you are agitated, you may find yourself taking rapid, short breaths. Allowing this shallow chest-only breathing to continue will aggravate your anger. Instead, take steps to refocus your breathing and relax your muscles in order to calm down. Try these breathing techniques to help manage your anger:

Breathing Slowly

Begin your relaxation attempts by taking several calm and deep breaths in succession, exhaling twice if you inhale. Slowly count to four while you inhale, and then slowly count to eight as you exhale. Take note of where the air in your lungs is traveling while you do this. Breathe deeply over the entire range of your lungs.

4-7-8 Deep Breathing

You may practice 4-7-8 breathing at any time and in any place. When you initially start out, try to practice at least twice a day, but you can do it as much as you like. In the beginning, only do four cycles in a row. After you have gotten used to it, you can work up to eight cycles. You could feel dizzy at first, but this will pass. Locate a comfortable seat with your back straight. Keep your tongue pressed on the back of your top teeth. Make a 'whoosh' sound as you exhale entirely through your mouth and around your tongue. If it helps, purse your lips. On the count of four, purse your lips and inhale through your nose. Hold your breath for seven counts. Exhale entirely through your lips for a count of eight, generating a whoosh sound. This concludes one cycle. Repeat for a total of three more rounds. When you're stressed, do 4-7-8 breathing. As you do it, it will get more powerful. It is suggested to practice this breathing technique before responding to an upsetting circumstance or when you are having difficulties relaxing.

By engaging your parasympathetic nervous system, the type of deep breathing done as part of the 4-7-8 breathing method helps to relax your body. Your autonomic nervous system oversees your body's automatic operations, such as heartbeat and digestion. The sympathetic nervous system and the parasympathetic nervous system are the two elements of this system.

Your body's stress reaction is controlled by the sympathetic nervous system. Your body's rest and relaxation responses are controlled by the parasympathetic nervous system. When one of these is turned on, the other is turned off; therefore, deep breathing is so good at inducing calm.

Alternate nostril breathing

Blocking one nostril while breathing with the other, rotating between the nostrils in an even pattern, is known as alternate breathing. To stay in shape, it's best to practice this breathing pattern while sitting. Bend your index and middle fingers into the palm of your hand, straightening your thumb, ring finger, and little finger. Close your eyes or look down gently. To start, inhale and exhale deeply. Block the right nostril by using your thumb. Inhale deeply through the left nostril. Using your ring finger, close the left nostril. Exhale through the right nostril by opening it. Inhale deeply through the right nostril. Use your thumb to close the right nostril. Exhale through the right nostril by opening it. Inhale deeply through the right nostril. Use your thumb to close the right nostril. Exhale through the left nostril, and open it. Inhale deeply through the left nostril. Increase the number of rounds you do this breathing rhythm to ten. Stop for a moment if you start to feel lightheaded by opening both nostrils and breathing normally.

Belly breathing

Find a tranquil and comfortable place to sit or lie down. Sitting in a chair, crossing your legs, or lying on your back with a small pillow under your head and another pillow beneath your knees are good options. Place one hand on your chest and the other on your stomach, just below your ribs. Let your stomach relax without straining or contracting the muscles to push it in. Inhale slowly through your nose. The air must go in through your nose and down, causing your abdomen to rise with one hand and draw inward against your spine with the other. Exhale slowly with slightly pursed lips. Pay attention to the hand on your chest; this hand will be quite still. Although the frequency of the sequence may vary depending on your health, most individuals start with three repetitions and gradually increase to five to ten minutes, one to four times each day.

Box breathing

Box breathing also referred to as four-square breathing, is a simple technique to learn and master. This form of timed breathing is already known to you if you've ever caught yourself inhaling and exhaling to the beat of the music. To a count of four, exhale. Hold your breath for four counts with your lungs empty. Inhale for four counts. Hold your breath for four counts. Exhale and restart the pattern.

Lion's breathing

Another beneficial deep breathing technique is the lion's breath, which involves sticking out your tongue and roaring like a lion. It can help you relax your facial and jaw muscles, relieve tension, and enhance your cardiovascular performance. The exercise is best done in a comfortable sitting position with your hands on your knees or the floor, leaning forward slightly. Stretch your fingers to the maximum. Inhale slowly and deeply through your nose. Extend your tongue down toward your chin by opening your mouth wide and sticking it out. Forcefully exhale, bringing your breath over the root of your tongue. Make a deep "ah" sound from deep within your abdomen while exhaling. For a few seconds, breathe normally. Repeat up to seven times.

Pursed-lip breathing

Pursed-lip breathing is a basic breathing technique that might help you take slower, more deliberate deep breaths. Relax your neck and shoulders by sitting in a comfortable position. Inhale softly via your nose for two seconds while keeping your mouth closed. Exhale for four seconds through your mouth, puckering your lips as if kissing someone. While breathing out, keep your breathing calm and steady. Experts advocate practicing pursed-lip breathing four to five times a day to get the proper breathing rhythm.

Resonance breathing

Coherent breathing, also known as resonance breathing, might help you relax and reduce anxiety. Close your eyes and lie down. Breathe in slowly via your nose, mouth closed, for six seconds. Don't overfill your lungs with air. Allow your breath to leave your body softly and gently for six seconds without straining it. Continue for a total of ten minutes. Spend a few more minutes being motionless and concentrating on how your body feels.

Simple breathing exercise

This easy breathing technique can be repeated as frequently as necessary. Standing, sitting, or lying down are all options. Stop for the time being if you find this exercise challenging or if you feel it is causing you anxiety or panic. Progressively increase the time the next time you try it again. Slowly and thoroughly inhale through your nose. Maintain a comfortable posture with your shoulders. Your stomach should grow, and your chest should only slightly lift. Slowly exhale through your mouth. Purse your lips slightly as you exhale, but maintain your jaw relaxed. As you exhale, you may hear a gentle "whooshing" sound. Carry on with the breathing practice; repeat for a few minutes or until you begin to feel better.

Have you tried any of the above breathing techniques, particularly after or before feeling enraged?

Yes   *No*

If you have, list down how this has helped you.

_____

_____

_____

_____

_____

Are you willing to start incorporating these into your daily schedule? I suggest you incorporate these in your morning stretch or as you mediate.

Yes   *No*

Yoga

yoga and meditation place such a high value on self-actualization. It is vital to understand what can happen if you lose control of your anger once you've acknowledged it. There are various yoga positions that might assist if your anger or tension is still spiraling out of control, and the below are just a few examples:

- Savasana, or Corpse Pose, is a very calming posture that is prized for its capacity to soothe both the body and the psyche. Lay on your back and place your arms relaxed at your sides and palms facing up to enter Savasana. Allow your feet to naturally expand and your breathing to return to its normal rhythm. Concentrate solely on the sound of your own breathing until you have reached a state of full relaxation.
- Child's Pose is excellent for building the mind-body connection and keeping you aware of our emotions. Child's Pose is another pose that is developed for relaxation and is aimed to quiet the muscles and mind. Begin by kneeling on all fours to enter Child's Pose. With your head lying on the ground, push back and bring your arms around to the sides of your body. Spread your

arms in front of you for a prolonged Child's Pose to stretch your shoulders.

- Half Sun Salutation to Plank Stance to a more relaxed pose like Savasana or Child's Pose is a beautiful three-part series of poses. For starters, stand tall with your feet together and your hands folded in front of your chest in the Half Sun Salutation as if you were praying. Sweep your arms up and focus on your fingers while inhaling, keeping your waist pulled outward. Exhale deeply and fold forward with your palms on the floor, keeping your head buried. Next, inhale deeply while putting your body into an upward forward fold. Finally, pull your arms back over your head, letting your hands touch. Plank Pose is a terrific way to finish the Half Sun Salutation. Holding a push-up stance is what Plank Pose is all about. Start with your hands parallel and shoulder-width apart, legs straight, and push up with your arms and core, making sure to activate your glutes. Hold this posture as long as you can. After that, finish off your practice with a relaxing stance like Child's Pose.

Describe how you felt after trying any of the above.

_____

_____

_____

_____

_____

Are you willing to start incorporating yoga regularly to help curb your anger issue? If yes, make sure you include this in your daily planner and make sure you leave time for this in your routine.

Meditation

Anger, fury, irritation, and resentment are all emotions that can be felt. These are all emotions that may appear to be impacted by outside factors. Your responses to events, people, and the environment can be impulsive at times. You might become enraged and worked up over something in a moment and not even realize it until it's too late. The truth is that you do have some influence over how you react to environmental stimuli. You manage how you respond and how long you allow yourself to remain angry or irritated. How often have you responded furiously to something, perhaps even physically, only to feel humiliated a few minutes later? More times than you can remember. You may become much more conscious of your sentiments of anger as they occur with regular meditation and better determine how you respond to situations as well as how long you stay furious. Meditation isn't about attempting to control or repress anger. We're all human, and we have innate reactions to things that irritate, disturb, or disappoint us. When you practice frequent guided meditation for anger, you can allow yourself to feel the emotion and then let it pass rather than lingering or exacerbating the emotion by reacting or responding in the incorrect manner.

Meditation is the deliberate practice of focusing one's attention on anything, such as breathing, an object, sound, movement, or sensation. Meditation is not about quieting or devoid the mind, contrary to common opinion; it's about training the mind to focus, directing the nervous system to naturally balance itself, activating the parasympathetic nervous system (PNS), and enabling the sympathetic nervous system (SNS) to settle down. Meditation may help you concentrate your mind, relax your body, and lessen fragmented thoughts and feelings, as well as the urges to act on them if you practice it regularly. Meditation can help you overcome your anger on several levels by addressing your underlying beliefs, feelings, and physiological responses. It promotes a peaceful, balanced calm by reducing our cognitive, emotional, and bodily reactions to rage. Meditation breaks the cycle of anger, suppresses our fight-or-flight response, and encourages emotional self-control. It rewires the brain and alters how we understand and respond to events that make us angry in the first

109

place. When you meditate, you calm the amygdala's activity, which turns off the instinctive stress response and reduces the synthesis and circulation of harmful stress chemicals like cortisol. Because of the brain's natural ability to adapt, develop, and expand, it may modify its reactions and habitual patterns of processing and connect to experiences. As a result, you may alter how you react to people, events, and ideas that make you angry. When practiced daily, meditation can help you stay focused on the present rather than becoming caught up in a negative thought loop. It improves your emotional awareness, reduces your inclination to react impulsively, and allows you to behave in ways that help you get to your goals. It fosters acceptance as well as the ability to tolerate and cope with discomfort. Meditation aids in broadening your viewpoint and releasing you from self-defeating automatic negative ideas like catastrophizing and all-or-nothing thinking, as well as strengthening your capacity to watch, remain detached, and notice what is occurring without judgment.

Different styles of meditation need different components to attain the desired results. Yoga and Tai Chi, for example, need a lot more room due to the movement involved, as opposed to a guided meditation or mantra meditation. Visualization or guided imagery meditation are other terms for guided meditation. It asks you to create a mental image of a place or circumstance that you could find pleasant while using all or as many of your senses, such as smell, sight, and hearing. Mantra meditation requires repeatedly repeating a word, a sentence, or a phrase to block out distracting ideas. Transcendental Meditation is a style of meditation in which you repeat a mantra that you choose in a certain manner. It enables your body to go into a deep state of relaxation as your mind strives for inner peace. Qi Gong is a synthesis of numerous ideas. It combines meditation, relaxation, physical activity, and breathing exercises with the goal of restoring and maintaining balance. Whichever type of meditation you pick, they all require a quiet surrounding and a comfortable position. Most importantly, you need to start this practice with an open and positive attitude. Through relaxed breathing techniques and maintaining focus, meditation can be a successful way to curb your anger. If you're just upset and can't seem to let go of it, meditation may be a useful technique for physically relaxing and mentally calming you. You may begin to look at your position and what is bothering you more sensibly now that you have a clear head, rather than letting your sentiments about the circumstance affect your response to it. Meditation may also be utilized to assist your de-stress when you are feeling particularly irritated or angry. You may utilize meditation to bring you back to a peaceful condition instead of concentrating your anger and energy on something you may regret later.

Here are a few meditation techniques for you to try:

Watch and follow

Allow your breath to take the lead in this meditation, giving your thoughts and emotions a respite. The relaxing pattern of your breath helps you to release tension and anger from your body and mind. It allows you to connect with the part of you that is not angry. Follow the steps below to get started: Slowly and deeply inhale, imagining a peaceful white light filling your entire body along with the fresh air you're breathing. As the white light comforts you, hold your breath for two counts, allowing your breath to collect sensations of stress and wrath. Slowly and thoroughly exhale, imagining the anger leaving your body along with your breath. As you exhale, notice how the tension in your body dissipates.

Release your anger

This meditation concentrates on bodily feelings and any stress you may have in your body. Anger manifests itself not just in our minds and emotions but also in our physical bodies. Focusing on the bodily manifestations of anger might help you become more aware of where you're keeping your anger and allow you to release it intentionally. Follow the steps below to get started: Focus your attention on your feet while you breathe; wriggle your toes, flex and point your feet; visualize your foot muscles releasing anger. Shift your focus to your legs. Imagine your legs releasing anger by squeezing and releasing the muscles in your legs. Now pay attention to your torso. As you inhale, imagine a soft, soothing wave sweeping away tension and anger from your entire chest and belly. Feel your neck and shoulders, then roll them a few times, squeezing them up to your ears and then releasing them down, letting them relax and release. Move your neck to release any angry knots. As you tension and relax your muscles, pay attention to your arms and hands. Curl your fingers forming fists and gently release them; gently shake them, visualizing anger and stress escaping as you do so. Concentrate on the muscles of your face and scalp; scrunch and release them to relieve tension and rage. Scan your body from head to toe again, squeezing and releasing any leftover tightness. Visualize the anger leaving your body and moving away from you.

Be an observer

Practice watching your thoughts and emotions in this meditation, expanding your awareness of them and allowing them to exist without judgment. Observe your thoughts and transfer your focus away from them to see whether your desire to act changes. Follow the coming steps below to get started with this. Choose a specific subject to concentrate on, such as the sound and sensation of your breathing or a fascinating object. Take note of sensory aspects such as sound, bodily sensations, textures, form, and so on. When your mind wanders, pay attention to the feelings that come. Keep those feelings in mind; how is your body reacting? Keep going with this experience; avoid the impulse to stop and act on your sensations; let them drift away as you restore your focus to your breath or object. As the temptation to respond fades, repeat the pattern of moving your attention between your emotions and your focal item.

Think in colors

Anger is often connected with the color red. Everything you see when you are furious is warped and stained in hues of crimson if rage were genuinely red. Visualizing colors in this meditation helps you adjust your viewpoint so you can see yourself and the world in their genuine hues rather than red. Follow the steps below to get started: Recognize your emotions by seeing the color red entering your body and coloring everything around you as you inhale and exhale. Pay attention to the sensations going on in your body as you do this. Imagine one of your favorite colors and take a deep breath in, allowing it to fill you up. Allow the color to saturate the space around you as you exhale. Imagine something pleasurable that you connect with that color and keep that image in your mind while you breathe in and out the color. As thoughts and feelings of rage enter your mind, visualize how this anger alters the colors you see. Inhale deeply to absorb this crimson rage; exhale to see it leave your body and dissipate. Return to inhaling your favorite color.

Be curious

Anger is perfectly normal to experience, but it has its limitations. It takes control of your ideas, feelings, and behaviors. Approaching it with curiosity can help you broaden your ideas and emotions, allowing you to achieve more equilibrium. Then you should be in a better position to make educated judgments on how to manage an enraged scenario. Be guided by the following steps to get started with this meditation. Allow yourself to feel angry; observe and recognize it in your thoughts and body at first. Allow anger to exist as you breathe, without trying to modify it or making plans to act on it. "And what else?" you might wonder. What else are you experiencing right now in your life? Other than stress, how do you feel in your body? Allow for it to live and grow. What do you see in your immediate surroundings? Allow your attention to gradually roam; take in what is around you without focusing too much on any one thing. What are the sounds you're hearing? Allow them to enter and exit your consciousness. Do you detect any doors? Allow your concentration to be with them as you breathe them in. Do you have any residual flavors in your mouth? Recognize when your mind wanders back to angry ideas and feelings. As you breathe, keep asking, "And what else?"

10 Minute guided meditation session

Sit on a floor cushion or find a comfortable chair to sit on instead. Place your hands in your lap and relax. Take a few deep breaths in a while, keeping your eyes open as you do this. We breathe in via our noses and out through our mouths. Close your eyes after roughly a minute. Bring your focus to your own body. Take note of your weight on the floor or on your chair. Take note of your physical points of touch, such as your feet on the floor, back on the chair, and hands in your lap. And simply focus your attention on this for a few moments. Now focus your attention on your breathing. Allow yourself to simply observe your

113

breath at this point. There's nothing you need to adjust or invent here; simply pay attention to the breath and its sensations. It might be the rising and falling feelings in the chest or stomach or the chilly inhale followed by the warm exhale. For a few seconds, focus your attention on this. If you're feeling angry right now, check if you can observe it without judging it. It is neither nice nor harmful; it simply exists. Keep an eye on this emotion as if it were simply another item you're paying attention to. Physically, where do you perceive this emotion? Is it lodged in your sternum? Is it your throat? Which comes first: your head or your abdomen? Perhaps there's some strain in the shoulders or chin. If you find your anger manifesting as a bodily experience, simply observe it. What happens to it after that? Is it moving? Does it go away? Also, if you sense any stiffness in your shoulders or jaw, try to relax your entire body. Any changes in your mood should be noted here. Now pay attention to your breathing. Return your focus to the breath if you notice your mind has wandered or become lost in thought, or even interacting with the anger you feel when thinking. Finally, slowly open your eyes. Take note of how you're feeling. If you're still furious, recognize it. Accept it and move forward. Keep an eye on it. If you're in a different mood, pay attention to it. Return to your day by taking a couple of deeper breaths.

Meditation is straightforward, but the most important thing to remember is that straightforward does not equate to easy. Knowing and remembering that it's natural for your thoughts to wander can help you be calm and patient while you educate your mind to focus and be centered. Begin by meditating for no more than five minutes. Meditation has a long list of advantages. Daily meditation is beneficial, but even a few times a week can suffice. Try to combine this with a habit you already have. Meditation may be included in a regular portion of your day, such as your wake-up or wind-down activities, to help you establish the habit and make it something you look forward to. You don't have to meditate in the typical cross-legged position. Respect your body by sitting or lying down in a comfortable position. You're giving your mind and body the time it needs to rest and de-stress during meditation, and you often feel drowsy afterward. If you're having trouble staying awake, consider adjusting your position or switching to a different time of day. Rather than putting hard guidelines on what your meditation practice should look like, be present in your experience and let it flow naturally. Self-criticisms should be noted and replaced with loving, forgiving thoughts. As you concentrate on one subject, be conscious of your thoughts. When your mind wanders, notice it and gently refocus it. Remember that meditation is not about emptying your mind of all ideas and emotions; it's about learning how to concentrate your attention on what you want to pay attention to so you can pick your responses and actions more carefully.

Positive thought has a lot of power. Begin to believe that you can reach pleasure, contentment, success, and inner peace. Expect good things if you keep your eyes on the sunny side of life. Most wars are fought in the head. Before you begin meditating, have faith that you will attain your goals. If you want to acquire a sane state of mind, believe in your ability to do so, and in the power of meditation will support you. It goes without saying that you cannot concentrate in an environment that is full of distractions. This includes having a large number of people around you, as well as noise and other distractions. Find a quiet location where you can hear both your thoughts and your breathing. This contributes to the success of the meditation practice. Breathing that includes the entire body is essential during meditation. Long, deep breaths are required. You should calm down and pace your breathing. Feel the oxygen traveling through your complete respiratory system, beginning with your nose and continuing via your trachea to your lungs. You can combine breathing techniques enlisted earlier during your meditation sessions. The fundamental goal of meditation is to relax your mind by clearing it of numerous distractions. Concentrate on a certain time, location, or situation, and avoid getting side-tracked by other ideas as much as possible. Meditation can help you learn how to break free from a cycle of self-harming behavior, conquer anxiety, heal insomnia, or simply allow yourself the time and space to relax and enjoy a moment of pure peace and quiet.

Here are some things that may be getting in the way of your meditation and its benefits:

Self-Criticism

This is typical among newcomers. You first believe you're doing everything incorrectly and that you're not paying attention to the results. When this happens, don't be too hard on yourself; instead, try to relax as much as possible.

Getting Tired

Few people can maintain such a calm mood without falling asleep or drifting off. This might be due to exhaustion or the fact that you are typically this relaxed shortly before going to bed, and your body has been trained to be that way. To avoid falling asleep, try meditating with your eyes open and maintaining an upright position, or go for a stroll.

Experiencing Pain

After a long duration of sitting in the same posture, this is particularly noticeable on your legs or back. You can adjust your posture and stance if this occurs.

Fear

The brain is not always the safest place to be. You may find yourself straying off to unpleasant ideas and circumstances when meditating. If this happens, take a deep breath and attempt to bring your thoughts back to your original focal point.

Which of these do you experience during meditation?

The following are some traditional approaches to meditation that are not compulsory, especially for beginners:

- Find a comfortable position to sit.
- You do not have to close your eyes by force if you do not want to.
- Place your hands on your thighs and try to relax.
- Concentrate on the region below your belly button.
- Breathe softly and evenly, counting each inhalation and exhalation from one to ten, then counting back to one.
- Allow your ideas to flow in and out. Do not concentrate on a single thought.

- If a thought interrupts your counting, concentrate on your breathing and resume again.
- Do this for approximately Twenty minutes.

After trying at least one of the meditation routines described above, write a little bit about how this had you feeling and how you think it has helped your anger.

_____

_____

_____

_____

_____

_____

_____

_____

_____

_____

_____

_____

_____

Physical activity

In principle, exercise is a terrific answer, but some individuals may find it difficult to devote their energy to a workout while they are angry. When you're angry or frustrated, there are several approaches to movement. Some people like to vent their frustrations through explosive activities like boxing, circuit training, or dance. Others may prefer mind-body exercises like yoga, Tai Chi, or meditation to calm their breathing and lower their heart rate. Some people may even like a mix of the two, such as going for a hike in the woods. It's also possible that what works on one occasion isn't as successful on another. So, keep an open mind and try a variety of activities to help you relax. Jumping rope, circuit training, aerobic activity, walking, and running are all examples of physical activities you can choose when you are angry, but not only. The health benefits of regular physical activity are well known, so the best suggestion is to incorporate it into your daily lives but choose to return to it more often when you are faced with an outburst of anger. While exercise is one strategy that many individuals use to lower their anger, other people may struggle to keep their emotions in check through physical activity, which can lead to disastrous outcomes. As a result, it's better to act before anger becomes a problem. If you need help controlling your anger, contact a mental health specialist or seek a referral from your healthcare practitioner.

The following are some ideas of physical activities you may want to start incorporating and how these will help with your anger:

- Researchers have identified aerobic activity as a technique to lessen anger expression in both children and adults, so you might want to work up a sweat to calm your tensions. Rowing and treadmill running has been linked to decreased levels of anger, depression, and anxiety.
- Workouts involving boxing need you to concentrate on certain punch and jab combinations. A boxing workout works the entire body, burns calories, and increases strength, particularly in the upper body. You may choose to attend classes in a gym or get a personal trainer. Of course, boxing at home is an option, and it does not require a large financial investment. You may buy

gloves and other boxing equipment, then use a smartphone app to train.

- Jumping rope is another high-intensity activity that needs attention and concentration. The positive thing about this workout is that it swiftly raises your heart rate and burns calories. It also necessitates the use of very minimal equipment. You can get a rope at a reasonable price. Jump rope workouts can include techniques like the double foot jump, running step, high step, or double under, which push you to focus on your feet instead of your anger.

- A circuit exercise is beneficial because it keeps you moving. You travel from station to station, working on different body parts for brief periods of time, so you do not leave much time to think about what's making you upset. Some basic equipment, like dumbbells, kettlebells, or resistance bands, may be required to complete a circuit at home. You might also do a whole bodyweight circuit, in which you just utilize your own body to create strength and sweat.

- Tai chi is a sort of martial art that originated in China, yet it is not hostile in nature. Instead, it's a succession of flowing motions and self-meditation. If you find yourself fired up and agitated, the gradual rhythm of the movement may help you calm down and lower your heart rate. There are several styles of tai chi, but there are online tai chi courses and smartphone applications that can assist you if you are just getting started.

- Walking has a number of health advantages, including improved cardiovascular health and a lower chance of chronic illnesses like type 2 diabetes. Walking can also be a good method to let off steam. A single session of walking for less than ten minutes was observed to lower anger and rage in young adults. Other studies found that among thirty-five overweight individuals who participated in a twelve-week walking program, attaining 10,000 steps per day led to lower levels of reported anger, as well as reduced anxiety, melancholy, weariness, disorientation, and overall mood distress.

- Getting outside and taking on more difficult terrain, such as woods, deserts, or steep ridges, is a terrific way to let go of tension and anger. Exposure to nature has been proved in studies to have a meaningful impact on your body. Exercising in natural settings is connected with enhanced emotions of renewal and positive involvement, decreased stress, confusion, anger, and despair, and improved vitality as compared to exercising indoors.
- Dance has been used to commemorate life, honor traditions, show joy, and convey anger for thousands of years. Dance movement therapy has been used successfully in cancer patients to treat feelings of loneliness, despair, anger, and fear, despite the fact that it has not been thoroughly investigated. There are many various ways to move and groove your body. You may move your body with breath, affirmations, or rhythm to release anger, whether you have a few minutes or an hour.

What physical activity from those listed above, or not, do you find mostly calms your anger?

_____

_____

_____

_____

Do you do this regularly?

Yes   *No*

Do you do this because you get angry often or because you feel like it calms you overall and helps with your next raging moment?

Physical activity should be a crucial part of everyone's life, especially if you are a woman who struggles with anger management. So, make sure you start incorporating this on the regular.

Self-care

Self-care goals vary by person, but in general, they include maintaining excellent mental and physical health, reducing stress, meeting emotional needs, maintaining romantic and platonic relationships, and finding a balance between one's personal and academic or professional lives. The word "self-care" refers to the steps that a person can take to achieve optimal physical and mental health. Self-care may also refer to activities such as meditation, writing, or seeing a counselor that an individual engages in to relax or achieve emotional well-being. Self-care might involve things like getting a haircut or a massage, going on a vacation, or dining at one's favorite restaurant, as well as taking care of one's essential necessities. Crafting, sketching, painting, writing poems or short tales, constructing something, and cooking are all good methods to let out your frustrations. Plus, you'll have a one-of-a-kind design on the opposite side! Our minds may be greatly influenced by music. When you're upset, listening to metal is likely to make you even more agitated. Instead, listen to music that makes you joyful and relaxed or music that you can dance to. You may even compose your own song! When coping with heavy emotions, it's easy to forget about hygiene, yet getting back to fundamentals may help us feel more human again. To unwind, spray cold water on your face or take a hot shower. Feeling angry or sad is a natural human emotion, but it may drain you physically and mentally, especially if you don't get enough sleep on a regular basis. When you just need a break from those who are annoying you, try taking asleep. Slow, deep breathing sends a signal to your brain that you're in a safe place, which can assist drop blood pressure and slow your heart rate. For a guided breathing experience, try anger meditations. Any game that requires you to engage with other people and obey rules might help you break free from your own thoughts. Play air hockey in the arcade, basketball with your siblings, or try out a new board game or video game. When you're attempting to relax, focusing on something outside of yourself will help. Whatever self-care approach you select, whether meditating on how beautiful the sky is, or becoming the reigning air hockey champion, know that the next time your rage seems out of control, you take good care of yourself in the face of strong emotion. Keep in mind that you have complete control over your words, actions, and behaviors.

What does self-care mean to you? Describe what activities mean self-care to you and think about how often you do these.

_____

_____

_____

_____

_____

_____

Cannabinoid products

Cannabidiol, also known as CBD for short, is the second most prevalent component of cannabis after THC. CBD is a non-intoxicating compound derived from the hemp plant. The World Health Organization (WHO) has announced CBD to be both safe and non-addictive. CBD has a variety of therapeutic applications, including the treatment of stress, anxiety, and depression. It also aids in the inhibition of seizures, the relief of pain, and the induction of sleep. The anti-stress properties of CBD are linked to its anxiolytic properties. Studies show that CBD helps manage stress, which helps control anger. CBD also produces pleasure chemicals in the body that can help with anger. As a result, these hormones promote relaxation, lower stress levels, and reduce anxiety. All these effects aid in the suppression of anger. CBD contains anti-inflammatory properties that assist in relaxing the body and alleviating discomfort. Pain and the deficits it causes might result in tension, despair, and worry. As a result, the patient is prone to get enraged in such situations. CBD can regulate anger indirectly by alleviating pain. CBD also possesses antipsychotic effects, which may aid in the treatment of illnesses such as schizophrenia and mood swings. It lowers anger by neutralizing the emotion. Frustration because of cognitive and sensory disability is another source of rage. CBD can assist with both issues, lowering the likelihood of an angry outburst. Sleep deprivation can also contribute to rage. As a result, CBD is beneficial since it has a sedative effect. In response to the topic of whether CBD can assist with anger, it's reasonable to state that CBD can help with problems like sleeplessness, anxiety, and depression, all of which may cause people to become irritable. As a result, CBD aids indirectly in the management of stress and other antecedents to rage. However, more research on CBD's effects on the body and brain is being conducted all the time. If you're thinking about using CBD, talk to your doctor first and make sure you are in line with your local regulations on such products.

Acupuncture

Chronic or acute stress, which results in energy stagnation, especially in the liver, is one of the most prevalent causes of rage, according to Traditional Chinese Medicine (TCM). The liver is in charge of maintaining a healthy flow of qi throughout the body. When qi becomes lodged in our bodies, emotions become locked as well, making them difficult to express or even recognize. Several methods, according to TCM, can aid the movement of qi and emotion in our bodies. Acupuncture is an excellent method for maintaining a healthy qi flow via the liver. Qi stagnation is fairly frequent, especially as you move out of the lower energy of winter and into the higher energy of spring. When qi is flowing freely, however, you can take advantage of all the opportunities that springtime has to offer. Seasonal acupuncture tune-ups are an excellent method to keep healthy throughout the year. Some persons with PTSD can benefit from acupuncture and other alternative treatments. Physical symptoms of PTSD, such as persistent pain and sleep difficulties, can be alleviated with these approaches. Acupuncture, herbal treatment, lifestyle, and dietary suggestions are used to treat irritability and moodiness caused by liver qi stagnation, with the goal of circulating qi and strengthening the liver and spleen organ systems. Additional investigations are needed to fully comprehend the relationship between acupuncture and anger management treatment; nevertheless, acupuncture has been effectively utilized to treat other emotional issues such as anxiety and depression. The theory of Chinese medicine and acupuncture is based on the idea that if your emotions are out of harmony, you will react in ways that are harmful to your general health. Correcting unstable or obstructed energy, based on this theory, can minimize the likelihood of a specific emotional condition like rage.

Chapter 16:
Things You Should Not Do When You're Angry

After listing everything, you SHOULD do when you get angry, here is a list of things you should NOT absolutely do.

- "Never go to bed furious," as the proverb goes, is sound advice. Negative emotions may be reinforced or preserved through sleeping. Sleep has been discovered to improve memory, particularly emotional memories. Sleep appears to aid in the processing and consolidation of knowledge acquired while awake. So, if you go to bed after an argument, that experience will most likely be more efficiently consolidated than if you stay awake for the next eight hours.

- Getting behind the wheel of a car when furious might be risky. According to studies, enraged drivers take greater risks and have more accidents. It's not a smart idea to get in a car while you're furious because you're poised for assault. Furthermore, anger causes tunnel vision, causing you to look straight ahead and miss a pedestrian or another car crossing the street in your peripheral view. If you must drive while furious, deliberately open your eyes and glance about to avoid tunnel vision.

- While getting your anger off your chest may seem like a good idea, it might really make things worse. People who spent just five minutes reading someone else's online complaints got angrier and less joyful. A study found that punching pillows to express anger not only enhanced anger at the time but also made violent conduct more likely in the future.

- Reaching for food to relieve your rage might backfire in a handful of ways. When you're irritated, you tend to eat unhealthy foods. Broccoli is never the first thing that comes to mind. People gravitate toward comfort meals that are heavy in sugar, fat, and carbohydrate. Furthermore, a high level of emotion triggers the fight or flight response, which makes the body believe it is in danger. Digestion suffers as a result of the "emergency" at hand and does not work efficiently. It's possible that you'll get diarrhea or constipation as a result of this.

- If you stay in the discussion while you're having trouble controlling your anger, you're more likely to say something you'll later regret. If you think you're going to say something terrible that you won't be able to take back, ask for a time out with the aim of returning to the conversation. It's possible that you'll require 10 minutes or ten days. The willingness to return to the dialogue and begin is crucial. Use the time to purposefully quiet your mind and body so you can express yourself more mindfully and intentionally.

- When you're furious, sharing your emotions with your friends and family on social media sites will almost certainly come back to haunt you. It is impossible to take something back after it has been made public.

- You can't take back an angry email after you've sent it; you can't take back a furious rant once you've sent it. If you can't stop yourself from putting down your furious thoughts, do it in a Word document. You won't be able to deliver it quickly this way, but you will be able to safely express your thoughts.

- After an enraged interaction, reaching for a glass of wine to de-stress typically has the opposite effect. Because alcohol impairs impulse control, it makes it more likely that you will act out your rage. Alcohol reduces inhibitions through acting on the frontal lobes of the brain, which oversee managing impulses that keep us from harming others or ourselves.

- Especially among past heart attack patients, the risk of heart attack increased by nearly five times, while the risk of stroke grew by three times. When you're furious, one of the wisest things you can do is check your blood pressure if you're prone to high blood pressure. When people feel furious, they should be aware of how their blood pressure changes. If it is increasing, they must work hard to control their anger through exercise, improved sleep, and physiological approaches.

- Rumination, or obsessively thinking about how the other person damaged you or was unjust to you, does not fix anything. If you find yourself on the other end of someone else's anger outburst, you might be able to calm them down by keeping your cool first. Begin by speaking to the furious individual in a tone that corresponds to his or her degree of anger, then gradually become calmer and steadier as you converse with them. They arrive in a more tranquil location as an outcome of this.

Given the above information, you should be well equipped for the next angry outburst, knowing what to do and what not to do.

From your experience, do you recall ever doing any of the above when getting enraged?

Yes   *No*

List these below:

_____

_____

_____

_____

From the numerous tips mentioned in this workbook so far, how can you change this?

_____

_____

_____

_____

Chapter 17:
Anger Q&A's

I n addition to the above valuable information, here are some common questions and quick answers in relation to anger:

What is the definition of anger?

Anger is a normal reaction to dangers that are considered to be real. It causes your body to release adrenaline, which tightens your muscles and raises your heart rate and blood pressure. Your senses may be sharper, and your cheeks and hands may flush. Anger, on the other hand, becomes an issue only when it is not managed properly.

Is it a terrible thing to be angry?

It isn't necessarily a terrible thing to be furious. Being enraged might assist you in communicating your problems. It can help you avoid being trampled by others. It may inspire you to take constructive action. The idea is to learn to control your rage in a healthy way.

What makes people angry in the first place?

Anger can be caused by a lot of factors, including loss of patience, feeling that your point of view and effort are not valued, and injustice. Anger can also be caused by memories of painful or upset experiences, as well as worries about personal problems. Based on what you were taught to anticipate from yourself, others, and the environment around you, you have your own set of anger triggers. Your personal background influences your angry emotions as well. If you were not taught how to express anger properly, for example, your emotions may simmer and make you miserable, or they could pile up until you explode in a furious rage. Inherited traits, brain chemistry, and underlying medical issues might all contribute to your anger outburst tendency.

In a nutshell, how should I react to anger?

When you're furious, you may deal with your emotions by expressing yourself. This is how you express your rage. A reasonable, sensible dialogue to a violent outburst is an example of expression. Suppression is an attempt to contain your rage so that it may be channeled into more productive conduct. Suppressing anger, on the other hand, might lead to you turning your anger within or expressing it via passive-aggressive conduct. By relaxing yourself and allowing your sensations to dissipate, you can manage your outer conduct and internal responses. In an ideal world, you'll select constructive expression, which involves expressing your worries and wants openly and directly without injuring or controlling others.

Is anger bad for my health?

According to studies, expressing anger incorrectly, such as holding it in, might be hazardous to your health. Suppressing anger tends to exacerbate chronic pain, whilst expressing anger appears to alleviate it. Anger and hostility have also been related to heart disease, high blood pressure, peptic ulcers, and stroke.

How do I know if my anger issues need professional help?

Learning to manage one's anger can be difficult for everyone at times. If your anger appears out of control, leads you to do things you regret, affects individuals around you, or is affecting your personal relationships, get therapy to manage it.

I am not sure what is causing my anger. What are the most common causes?

Anger is triggered by a variety of factors. Every person has a unique reaction to certain situations. This means that certain things may irritate someone while having no impact on you, and vice versa. As a result, a variety of similar causes can elicit anger in the majority of people. Situations in which one feels attacked, settings in which one feels helpless, disrespectful situations, stress, financial issues, alcoholism, and other mental diseases such as depression, to name a few. If you are currently experiencing one or more of these things and you feel you get angry often, you may have started to identify the triggers, as discussed earlier in the book.

These are quick and easy replies to the above questions, but further detail about each and every one of these is further discussed throughout the book.

Conclusion

It's considered that the release of tension that leads to acts of aggressiveness when we're angry is stress-relieving. Screaming, yelling, slamming doors, and hurling objects are all thought to have the same venting effect. Getting a "no" from your employer on a project you really wanted to accomplish, receiving criticism, or going through a severe breakup may all make you angry. You may be trembling because of your fury. It's possible that your heart is racing, your ears are ringing, and you're sweating, hot, and flushed. You are unable to think straight, but you are certain that you must punch something. You slam your fist against a wall instead of a person. The problem is that striking a wall isn't a viable option. At the same time, it may or may not provide a cathartic release of tension in the short term, which is why some mental health treatment clinics offer kickboxing as means of therapy if nothing changes in terms of your anger management problems. Instead of indulging in activities that result in cracked hands and issues with the police, there are undoubtedly other methods to relieve your fury and sadness.

Anger takes away a person's peace of mind, healthy intimacy with others, personal and professional stability, and even their life expectancy. According to research, chronic anger may impair a person's health in a variety of ways, as well as their personal and professional relationships. People who feel anger on a regular basis, for a short period of time, and as an appropriate response to specific conditions are unlikely to develop health problems or long-term interpersonal problems. Sustained, severe, and regular anger, on the other hand, can be troublesome for people on many levels. Anger may sap your vitality while consuming your attention and clouding your judgment. It can also lead to despair and drug misuse, among other mental health issues. Anger causes a spike of adrenaline in the body, as well as a faster heartbeat, higher blood pressure, and greater muscular tension in the form of clenched jaws or fisted fists. This can have a negative significance on your health over time and lead to physical ailments. Anger might make it difficult to concentrate at school or at work, affecting your performance. It can also have a negative impact on your connections with your peers. While creative disagreements, constructive criticism, and healthy arguments may be beneficial, lash outs, or emotional outbursts can alienate your peers and lead to bad consequences. Anger does the most harm to loved ones and can have a negative impact on your relationships with them. It can make individuals uncomfortable in your presence, diminish their trust and respect, and be especially harmful to youngsters. Anger has a negative impact on your work, relationships, and physical and mental well-being.

Anger management is a technique for coping with the emotional and physiological arousal that comes with anger. Because you can't always alter the events or people that make you angry, anger management helps you discover what your triggers are and learn to deal with them more effectively. While anger management is a type of treatment that aims to help you control your anger, unlike depression or anxiety, anger is not a medical disorder that can be diagnosed or characterized. Intense, destructive, or uncontrollable rage, on the other hand, can cause severe anguish and impairment, as well as jeopardize one's safety. Individuals who have difficulty acknowledging they have anger issues and taking responsibility for their behavior frequently blame others. They are having difficulties recognizing the situation as their fault. Something or someone is constantly to blame. Their outbursts of rage are usually attributed to something else. These people may benefit from some anger management classes. They must, however, embrace their behaviors and emotions for what they are: rage. When it is stated that they have an anger issue, many find it insulting. It is their lack of acceptance that keeps them from getting treatment; this will eventually lead to great difficulties such as the loss of a career. Although anger is not a diagnosable condition, it may be unexpected and difficult to manage. If left untreated, it will have negative repercussions on people's relationships and possibly lead to legal problems or jail. Friendships and family members may be harmed, and personal and professional relationships may be shattered because of violent outbursts. If your anger is placing you or others in danger of interfering with other elements of your life, it may be an indicator that you need to seek professional treatment. It's not something to be ashamed of. The sooner you get assistance, the better. Managing how you express your anger is a crucial skill for living in harmony with others. It is necessary for dispute resolution. Others will frequently withdraw and avoid you if they don't trust you to speak to them calmly and reasonably. Allowing our anger to manifest itself in furious words and voices is neither constructive nor healthy. Anger is a completely natural feeling that everyone should be allowed to experience at times when it is acceptable. When people routinely express themselves via anger when they should be expressing other emotions, the problem occurs, such as sadness, fear, joy, or embarrassment. When numerous emotions are channeled via the emotion of anger, the person becomes furious far more often than is healthy. As a result, if someone has anger difficulties, it suggests they have underlying mental or emotional issues that they are unable to cope with or process in a healthy manner. Instead, they become enraged toward them on a regular basis.

Anger, as you may know, is a tough emotion to regulate, especially when it feels strong and out of control. It's a good idea to learn beneficial anger management strategies rather than turning to harmful habits to try to lessen or forget them. Simple things like exercise, mindfulness, and finding someone you can talk to about your problems are all included in this workbook. It might feel like a lengthy journey at times. Something will eventually click, and you'll discover a few strategies that work for you. You have heaps of information that you can use as you please, and a combination of these approaches will surely control your anger temperament. Working on yourself, being conscious of all the positive things around you, and reducing the negative surrounding you, such as avoiding certain individuals and circumstances, are all things you can do. Because anger is frequently the result of poor self-esteem, increasing your self-esteem may and will improve your capacity to regulate your anger. It's better to let your anger out than to keep it within, but you should always attempt to do so quietly and without getting defensive or violent.

Excessive anger sufferers are also more prone to be clinically depressed or nervous. Why? Anger destroys relationships with family, friends, and co-workers, among other things. It has a bad impact on every aspect of one's life. Because of the humiliation or sorrow, they experience after acting out, many teenagers with anger issues have low self-esteem. However, it might also go the other way, with anger becoming a sign of despair. As a result, it should be evident that anger can be harmful to one's health. Anger should be addressed if it is or becomes an issue. With such a resourceful workbook at hand, you have everything you need to know to start managing your anger and turn your life around.

Author's Note

Dear reader,

I hope you enjoyed my book.

Please don't forget to toss up a quick review on amazon, I will personally read it! Positive or negative, I'm grateful for all feedback.

Reviews are so helpful for self-published authors and your feedback can make such a difference for my book!

Thanks very much for your time, and I look forward to hearing from you soon.

Sincerely,

Victoria

Made in the USA
Las Vegas, NV
02 January 2024

83804151R00075